Robert A. Hatcher, MD, MPH
Professor of Gynecology and Obstetrics
Emory University School of Medicine

Shannon Colestock, MS
Family Therapist
Steininger Center

Erika I. Pluhar, PhD
Project Director
Emory University Rollins School of Public Health

Christian Thrasher, MA
Program Manager and National Heath Educator
The 100 Black Men of America

Illustrated by **Regina Espino**
Atlanta College of Art '03

Cover design by **Digital Impact Design, Cornelia, GA**

Layout by **Anna Poyner**

Visit us @www.managingcontraception.com

i

ABOUT THE AUTHORS

Robert A. Hatcher grew up in Douglaston, Long Island, attended the Trinity School on Manhattan, Williams College, Cornell Medical School and the University of California at Berkeley (Masters in Public Health). He is a professor of gynecology and obstetrics at Emory University School of Medicine in Atlanta, GA. Bob has been the senior author of 17 editions of *Contraceptive Technology*. His hobbies include gardening (33 years) and golf (2 years). His wife, Margaret, is a creative interior designer and avid gardener. They have 5 children and 3 grandchildren. One of Bob's favorite rules of life: Live life in day-tight compartments!

Shannon Colestock lived in the back of his truck for two years to finish his undergraduate degree at Prescott College. He then earned a Masters degree in Human Sexuality Education from the University of Pennsylvania. Currently, he works at the Steininger Center as a family therapist working with families in crisis. His passions include judo, cooking, flirting, and spending time with friends, family, his wonderful partner Claudette, and their hilarious pug Basho. Claudette loves yoga and is a family therapist who specializes in helping families with adopted children. Basho's passions include lying in the sun, stealing panties, eating, and snuggling.

Erika I. Pluhar was born and raised in Michigan. She attended Cornell University where she was a member of the rowing team, and received her Ph.D. in Human Sexuality Education from the University of Pennsylvania. Her dissertation research was on mother-daughter communication about sexuality. Currently, Erika directs an HIV prevention study in the Rollins School of Public Health at Emory University and teaches a graduate course in human sexuality. She lives with her best friend and husband, Tyler, and their dog Lady. She loves cycling, camping, and hiking in the north Georgia mountains.

Christian Thrasher grew up in East Aurora, a suburb of Buffalo, New York. While completing a double major in radio production and psychology, Chris produced a sexuality based radio call-in show in Buffalo. After completing his Bachelors degree Chris moved to New York City where he attended New York University and received a Masters degree in Sexuality Education. While in New York City, he worked with Dr. Judy Kuriansky on her nationally syndicated call-in radio show "LovePhones." Chris now resides in Atlanta, Georgia with one of the few individuals who truly "gets him," his life partner and wife, Leslie. He works as a Program Manager and National Health Educator for the 100 Black Men of America, Inc. His hobbies include cooking and eating good food, playing golf, and talking about sex both on and off the airwaves.

Published and distributed in the United States by:
BRIDGING THE GAP COMMUNICATIONS, INC.
P.O. Box 888
Dawsonville, GA 30534
Phone: (706) 265-7435
Fax: (706) 265-6009
info@managingcontraception.com

How to order additional copies:
Refer to the order form in the back of this book for quantity discounts. You may also order direct from our website:
http://www.managingcontraception.com

Printed in the United States of America.

www.managingcontraception.com

DEDICATION

This book is dedicated to Dr. Judy Kuriansky, clinical psychologist and sex therapist. Dr. Judy, a world reknowned radio and TV personality whose credits include the nationally syndicated call-in show, "LovePhones," is a pioneer in the field of sexuality. She is the author of five books on sexuality and relationships, including *Generation Sex, How to Love a Nice Guy, The Complete Idiot's Guide to Dating*, and *The Complete Idiot's Guide to Healthy Relationships*. She works extensively in Japan and China on health and women's issues, and is on the advisory board of several magazines and public service organizations.

I met Dr. Judy in 1996 in her office at Premiere Radio Networks in New York City. There was never a formal introduction, but when she came through the door with an energy that lit up the room with just her smile. Only a week later, I found myself on the road with Dr. Judy as she toured colleges and universities throughout the northeast, discussing sex, love, dating and relationships with the students. She always communicated with young people in a way that eliminated the many stigmas around talking openly and honestly about sex, normalized their concerns, and gave them permission to ask questions and get information.

Over the next few years, I worked with Dr. Judy on "LovePhones" and learned an incredible amount about sexuality and the media. I saw how she, in a genuinely caring manner, helped people around the world learn and communicate about sexuality. She is a power of example in my life and emanates incredible energy wherever she goes. She has contributed greatly to the field of sexuality in her writing, speaking, and through every life she has touched on the radio and beyond. It is with great honor and pride that we dedicate the third edition of *Sexual Etiquette 101* to Dr. Judy Kuriansky.

—Christian Thrasher, MA

ACKNOWLEDGEMENTS

The authors would like to acknowledge all of the friends and family members—too numerous to list—whose support and love made work on this book possible. We would like to give a special thanks to the following people: Maxine Keel, for her commitment to family planning and sexuality education and for keeping everyone—especially Bob— organized; Laurie Bazemore, for her hard work and dedication to this and other BTG projects; Sarah Ivy Gibb, for her great ideas on the sexuality and spirituality section; Lydia Sausa, for excellent suggestions on gender identity and the trans community; Brook Brandon for careful editing; and the late Ceecee ("Moonie"), whose presence inspired the humorous song, "We Love You, You Love Us."

FORWARD

Sexual Etiquette 101 and More comes just at the right time! Recently, the Surgeon General released a long-awaited report encouraging Americans to respect "a diversity of sexual values," to recognize scientific knowledge about sexual issues, and to engage in open discussion about sexuality.

This book answers that "Call to Action to Promote Sexual Health and Responsible Behavior." It gives readers detailed and accurate information about how to make responsible sexual choices today by taking them through all the steps that are necessary to do that – from developing self-esteem, encouraging communication, practicing safe sex, understanding sexual problems and establishing healthy loving relationships.

As a clinical psychologist, certified sex therapist, radio call-in advice host, television commentator, newspaper and magazine advice columnist, and lecturer about sexuality for over a quarter of a century, you could say I have "heard it all." I've heard questions from men and women of all ages from all over our country and abroad, about love and sex. No matter what the specifics of the question have been, two deeper issues underlie the problem; everyone worries whether they are normal, and everyone wants to find the love they want. The answers lie in giving people support, accurate information and respect, and encouraging them to be responsible. *Sexual Etiquette 101* does this!

The answers also lie in quality sex education. *Sexual Etiquette 101* makes this point clear! With all the controversy in this country today about the specifics of sex education, there is one indisputable fact: sex education is necessary in order to overcome not just sexual problems suffered by Americans of all ages, but to ensure healthier kids, improve people's quality of life, and help everyone establish loving relationships.

It gives me great pride to know that my intern on my radio advice show, Christian Thrasher, has co-authored this book. From the early days of his involvement at my radio show, and traveling with me to lectures on college campuses around the country, I learned first-hand his commitment to this subject, sparkled with a wonderful cama-raderie and good humor. Those personal qualities are an important addition to dedica-tion when it comes to dealing with the field of sexuality, in order to make messages about responsible sexuality accessible to the broad public and especially to young peo-ple. My subsequent work with the intelligent, hard-working and delightful Erika Pluhar on a research project was a further pleasure and affirmation of hope that with such young professionals, the future of sex education is in capable hands.

Judy Kuriansky, Ph.D.
Adjunct Professor of Psychology, Columbia University Teachers College
Author, *The Complete Idiots Guide to Dating*

TABLE OF CONTENTS

CHAPTER 1:
Introduction

What is Sexual Etiquette?

There is not one "best" way to be sexual. Every culture, family, and couple has their own guidelines to being sexual. The guidelines of some cultures are rigid and strict while others are more flexible and accepting. What is expected or acceptable in one is not necessarily acceptable in another. In many ways, sexuality is like dancing. In some cultures you can dance with yourself. In some cultures you can dance with people of the same gender. In some cultures you cannot dance at all. In some cultures you can "grind" and dance passionately. Each one has different guidelines and taboos. None of the guidelines are better or worse, as long as everyone involved is consenting to the dance.

Just as all cultures are different, so, too, are individuals. We each have different needs, expectations, fantasies, turn-ons, turn-offs, feelings, and so forth. Despite the fact that we are all so unique and diverse, this book is written with the belief that there are certain universal values that may enable individuals to function and interact respectfully with other people. It is also designed to help people avoid and prevent certain behaviors that would hurt, disrespect, alienate, abuse, violate, or otherwise take away the rights of human beings to celebrate themselves. The information contained in the following pages will provide you, the reader, with more tools and skills to avoid the potentially negative side of sexuality while simultaneously helping you enjoy and embrace the potentially wonderful and positive side of sexuality!

The following guidelines will help identify some of the behaviors and attitudes that may contribute to more cultural and individual sexual health and well-being.

Guidelines for Sexual Etiquette

- We are all sexual. We each have a right to choose how to express our sexuality. Some people choose to be celibate, or only to kiss and hug while others choose to have intercourse. We each must choose for ourselves what is right for us.
- All people have value and worth and deserve to be treated with respect and compassion regardless of sex, gender, age, culture, sexual orientation, weight, race, physical ability, religion, and other traits.
- Relationships should be consensual. Consent is when everyone involved agrees with what is happening. It is not possible to give consent when impaired with alcohol or other drugs. Consent also includes respecting and honoring people's right to change their minds or say "no" at any time. As long as everyone is in agreement with the behaviors, feel free to have fun and enjoy one another's company!

1

- Physical or psychological abuse, violence, or coercion are never acceptable in any relationship.
- If you do not feel comfortable enough to discuss the behaviors in which you engage or want to engage, you may not be prepared for those behaviors.
- Honesty is the best policy! Lying tends to result in hurt feelings, miscommunication, misunderstanding, more lies, and a lack of trust. For open and honest communication to occur, the parties involved must be open to hearing what others have to say.
- Everyone deserves to be provided with reliable and accurate information about their bodies, health, and sexuality in developmentally appropriate ways.

Let's Talk About Sex!

Sexual messages are everywhere in our culture. We are bombarded with media messages and images. Every day on television, billboards, the radio, and in magazines we are exposed to sexual innuendos, jokes, rumors, and depictions of sexual behavior. Most of these messages seldom—if ever—address feelings, intimacy, using contraception, communication, or expectations. We usually witness sex as just happening with no communicating about it. If sex is brought up at all it, is usually on a sit-com where some uncomfortable parent makes a joke out of "the talk" with their child. We rarely witness a healthy and mature conversation between a child and a role model or adult mentor! We need more examples and traditions of healthy and open communication.

We are also commonly met with silence about these subjects from the adults and role models in society. We are given subtle messages that sex and sexuality are not to be discussed. Growing up, we are taught which topics are okay to discuss, which ones will get us a look of discomfort or nervous laughter, and which ones may get us in serious trouble. While the media continues to display an infinite array of sexual messages (usually with irresponsible examples), the adult community continues to perpetuate a culture of silence. Meanwhile, the young people get stuck in the middle by receiving very little genuine or meaningful communication and answers to their questions!

We must begin to view sexuality as much more than sex or "doing it." It's time to talk about the vastness of topics that make up sexuality. Sometimes when people hear "sexuality" they have trouble getting past the "sex" part of the word. Sex is a <u>small</u> part of sexuality. Sex includes physical acts that we do with our body, while sexuality is an umbrella term for the numerous topics, concepts, and ideas included in this book— from hygiene to body image, from love to loneliness, from our relationship with ourselves to our relationships with others...sexuality goes far beyond "sex." For example, someone may not be having intercourse and may still struggle with many sexuality issues such as intimacy, body image, depression, friendship, guilt, popularity, and so forth. In fact, perhaps a better name for this section would be "Let's Talk About <u>Sexuality</u>!"

Often, when people finally discuss sexuality, they address sexual assault, pregnancy, anatomy, emotional trauma, and sexually transmitted infections. If these were the only topics that made up sexuality, it would be a dark and depressing subject. In reality, sexuality is made up of a variety of issues that can be both beautiful or traumatic, ugly or spectacular. This makes it complicated because it is not easily classified as all good or all bad. That is why this book exists! This book will help to examine and make sense of the dark side, the wonderful side, and the various interpretations of sexuality. All of this makes sexuality a worthy study. Congratulations on taking the time and energy to learn about sexuality!

Let's Talk About Sex

My girlfriend and I are very open about talking about sex and our sexuality. Being open has brought us closer than I thought, and now having sex has become more enjoyable and less tense. Just talking about sex has made all the difference. Torrence, 23 years old.

Talking Beforehand Makes a Difference

I am 19. My boyfriend and I are each other's first partners. He is 21. We began having intercourse when I was 18. Not getting pregnant was very important to me. One of the reasons I chose my boyfriend as a partner is because he is so understanding and patient. He waited until I felt ready to have intercourse. Even before we decided to do "it" we discussed a wide variety of contraceptives – condoms, the pill, diaphragm, cervical cap. We decided on condoms and the pill. We began discussing contraception one year before we started having sex. We both pay for them and we both go to the health center together to get them. I think discussing contraception helped me feel more comfortable and relaxed about having intercourse, because we both could talk openly and knew how to protect ourselves...we knew the risks. Angela, 19 years old.

CHAPTER 2:
Relationship With Yourself

The most important relationship you will ever have will be with yourself. How you feel about yourself will powerfully affect the relationships you have with others and the decisions you make about your life. A person with self-love and self-respect may make very different decisions than someone who feels they are unworthy of love and respect from others. We hope this book will help you get in touch with your values, assess whether you are making decisions that are in line with your values, and, if necessary, help you make positive changes in your life.

Sexual and Reproductive Anatomy

Typically when we learn about sexuality, we are taught only about the biological aspects of sex. Somehow it is all right to talk about sex if we keep it scientific, but the psychological and emotional aspects of sexuality are often considered taboo. Nevertheless, anatomy is an important part of being a sexual person. This chapter is designed to help you get to know your sexual anatomy.

FEMALE REPRODUCTIVE ANATOMY

The external female sexual and reproductive anatomy includes:

VULVA – A collective term for the external female sexual anatomy. The vulva is made up of the mons pubis, clitoris, labia majora, labia minora, urethral opening, and vaginal opening.

MONS VENERIS – Derived from the term "Mountain of Venus," the mons veneris (or mons pubis) is the soft, fatty, triangular shaped pad of tissue covering the pubic bone. The mons pubis is covered with pubic hair after puberty.

CLITORIS – The organ at the top of the labia (above the vaginal and urethral openings). The only known functions of the clitoris are sexual stimulation, enjoyment, and pleasure. During sexual arousal, the clitoris fills with blood (similar to the penis) which can lead to orgasm. The clitoris is a complex structure comprised of the clitoral hood, glans, shaft and clitoral legs, which extend backward on either side of the urethra (see diagram). The urethral sponge, networks of nerves and blood vessels, as well as suspensory ligaments also make up the clitoris. By the way, did you know that the clitoris has a much higher density of nerve endings than the penis?

Adapted from: *Francoeur, R. (1995). The Complete Dictionary of Sexology. New York: Continuum Publishing Company.*

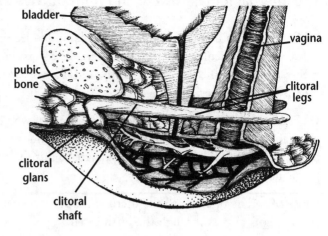

LABIA MAJORA – Two long, lip-like pads of skin, one on either side of the vaginal opening outside the labia minora.

LABIA MINORA – Two folds of skin between the labia majora, which extend from the clitoris on both sides of the urethral and vaginal openings.

URETHRAL OPENING – A small opening through which urine passes from the urethra.

VAGINAL OPENING (or, in some girls and women, HYMEN) – The opening leading to the vagina, through which menstrual fluid passes and through which a newborn passes during birth. In young girls, a thin membrane called the hymen usually covers the vaginal opening. Activities such as bicycling or horseback riding, tampon use, or sexual intercourse cause the hymen to stretch or tear.

BARTHOLIN'S GLANDS – Small glands on either side of the vaginal opening that secrete a small amount of fluid during sexual arousal.

ANUS – The opening from the rectum through which feces pass. It consists of two sphincters, one voluntary and one involuntary that can be relaxed and contracted.

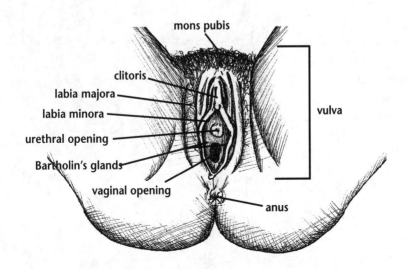

The internal female sexual and reproductive anatomy includes:

VAGINA – The highly expandable, tubular organ leading from the uterus to the vulva. It is a muscular structure that serves as an exit channel during monthly menses, is the birth canal during birth, and is involved in sexual intercourse and other sexual activities.

UTERUS – or womb, is a hollow, muscular organ where a fetus develops during pregnancy. The internal walls of the uterus, or endometrium, are rich with tiny blood vessels that fill with blood to prepare to nurish and support a fetus during pregnancy.

CERVIX – The opening to the uterus. The cervix expands during childbirth to allow a fetus to pass through the birth canal.

UTHERA – The tube through which urine passes out of the body from the bladder.

BLADDER – The organ that holds urine.

OVARIES – The pair of female gonads that produce eggs and female hormones (estrogen and progesterone). The ovaries are located in the abdominal cavity and are attached to the uterus and fallopian tubes.

FALLOPIAN TUBES – Narrow tubes through which a fertilized egg travels from the ovary to the uterus.

THE "G" SPOT –

Although some experts continue to debate its existence, we will define and point out the G-Spot. Named after the German doctor Ernst Grafenberg, the "G" spot is located in the anterior (front) wall of the vagina, just under the bladder, about two inches into the vagina. In some women, stimulation of this area produces the urge to urinate, followed by intense sexual arousal, which may lead to an orgasm. The "G" spot may be associated with female ejaculation (see page 22).

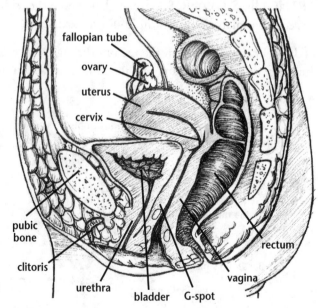

MALE REPRODUCTIVE ANATOMY

The external male sexual and reproductive anatomy includes:

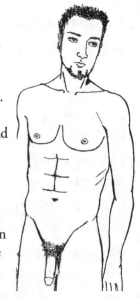

PENIS – The male organ through which sperm and urine pass. The penis is made up of the base (the part that attaches to the pelvis); the shaft (the body of the penis); and the glans (the head of the penis with the urethral opening at the tip). The corpus spongiosum and corpus cavernosa comprise the main internal structures of the penis. These spongy structures fill with blood to create an erection.

FORESKIN – In an uncircumcised male the foreskin is the thin layer of skin that covers the glans, or head, of the penis. As the penis becomes erect, the foreskin is stretched back, exposing the head of the penis.

SCROTUM – The loose pouch containing the testes, epididymis, and parts of the spermatic cords. The scrotum is attached to the body with muscles that contract and relax, pulling the testicles close to the body or moving them away in order to control their temperature.

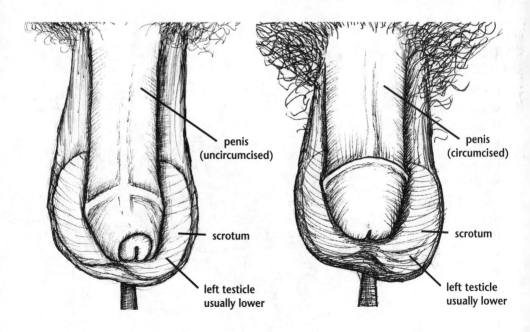

penis
(uncircumcised)

scrotum

left testicle
usually lower

penis
(circumcised)

scrotum

left testicle
usually lower

The internal male sexual and reproductive anatomy includes:

TESTES – The paired male reproductive glands that produce sperm and the hormone testosterone. The testes are loaded with nerves and are sensitive to touch and pressure.

EPIDIDYMIS – A tightly coiled "tube" (if stretched out, it would be 15- to 19-feet long!) where sperm produced by the testes are stored and become mature.

VAS DEFERENS – The tubes that transport sperm from the epididymis to the seminal vesicle and the prostate gland.

SEMINAL VESICLE – A pair of glandular sacs which secrete the fluid that makes up about 60% of ejaculate.

PROSTATE GLAND – A golf ball-sized structure that produces about 30% of the fluid in ejaculate. Prostate fluid helps to liquefy sperm.

COWPER'S GLANDS – Two pea-sized glands at the base of the penis located under the prostate. The Cowper's glands produce and secrete a clear fluid during sexual arousal known as pre-ejaculatory fluid or "pre-cum." This fluid can contain some viable sperm.

BLADDER – The organ that stores urine.

URETHRA – The tube through which urine and ejaculate pass.

ANUS – The opening from the rectum through which feces pass. It consists of two sphincters, one voluntary and one involuntary that can be relaxed and contracted.

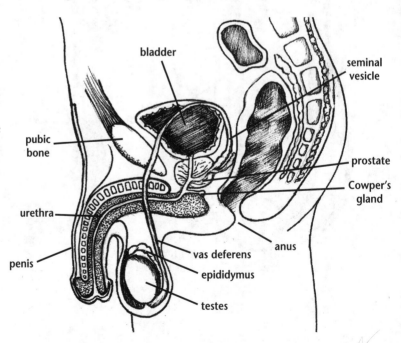

bladder

seminal vesicle

pubic bone

prostate

Cowper's gland

urethra

anus

penis

vas deferens

epididymus

testes

Self-esteem

Oscar Wilde once wrote, "to love oneself is the beginning of a lifelong romance." Such "self-love" centers on self-esteem. Self-esteem is a term that often gets used without much explanation.

- *"Self-esteem is most important."*
- *"It all comes down to self-esteem."*
- *"It he had better self-esteem, he wouldn't do that."*
- *"I like someone who has high self-esteem."*

However, although it's easy to say self-esteem is important, it can be tough to actually develop and maintain positive self-esteem. In fact, many people think negatively about themselves a lot of the time. You will probably feel different ways about yourself throughout your life, but it's your underlying sense of self that matters most.

Having positive self-esteem affects all aspects of life. People with more positive self-esteem are able to communicate their desires and needs to others more effectively. They think good thoughts about themselves and are able to both see and feel happy about the positive components of their lives. When things go wrong, they are able to figure out solutions, garner support of those around them, and cope with stressful situations.

Self-esteem is not the same as selfishness. Selfishness is wanting things for yourself without taking others (or the consequences) into consideration. Self-esteem is having a positive image of yourself and loving who you are. Having good self-esteem often is related to being able to see beyond yourself and to help and care for other people.

How is self-esteem related to sexuality? In just about every possible way! Sexuality is a fundamental part of a person. It involves body parts and processes as well as powerful emotions, such as lust and love. Not feeling good about your body, being unable to be vulnerable with or express your emotions to another person, and denying your sexual feelings can be related to having low self-esteem. In contrast, a person with positive self-esteem will tend to make sexual decisions that are in line with his or her values, have safer sex, and feel good about expressing sexual pleasure in a mutually respectful and caring manner.

So, how does one develop positive sexual self-esteem? Well, it's certainly not something that happens overnight. Developing self-esteem, sexual or otherwise, takes time and work. But there are some things that will help along the way. For example, getting to know your body through the resources in this book and through self-exploration helps you get in touch with yourself. Examining your sexual values can help you better understand the choices you make and will hopefully lead you to make future choices that are in line with your values. People also can learn about themselves and grow emotionally as well as sexually through positive relationships with other people. Finally, some people see mental health professionals to help develop self-esteem.

Self-esteem in Relationships

I've been in two relationships where the other people had really low self-esteem. It was hard on me and on the relationship. It's hard to tell right away how a person feels about themselves. But being with people who were always down on themselves eventually brought me down. I tried to change my past partners' feelings to make them feel better, but it didn't work. We just ended up getting in fights. I finally met someone recently who is confident and happy. It's like being in a different world when I'm with this person. It's such a relief and our relationship is so much better. James, 23 years old.

Taking Care of Myself

I have had four sexual partners. I have abstained from sex for the past six months. I really don't want to have sex for a while. I have promised myself that I need to feel better about me and who I am. Therefore, I won't do anything that could hurt me. Kimberly, 20 years old.

Sex in Search of Happiness

I had my first sexual encounter in the seventh grade. I had very low self-esteem, because I was gaining weight. My friends were having sex and they were happy, so I tried it to see if it would make me happy, too. It didn't. Meredith, 18 years old.

Depression: Don't Suffer in Silence

Depression is one of the most common mental disorders. It affects 340 million people in the world today and counts for 10% of productive years lost throughout the world. Depression is a mood disorder that may occur only once in a person's lifetime, or in "episodes" that can last from 9-16 months. Depression includes both mood disorders and anxiety disorders.

The causes of depression are complex and not yet fully understood. Researchers have identified biochemistry, genetics, social and environmental factors, certain medical illnesses, personality factors, and some medications as possible contributing factors to depression.

About half of all cases of depression go undiagnosed and untreated. Along with missed days at work or school, isolation and loneliness, trouble in interpersonal relationships, and other life problems, depression also can lead to suicide.

The good news, however,m is that depression is one of the most treatable mental illnesses. Below are listed some of the major symptoms of depression. If you or someone you know is experiencing these symptoms, seek help. You do not have to suffer in silence. There are many effective treatments available to help. Check out the resources below and in Chapter 10 of this book for more information.

Major Symptoms of Depression:
1. Depressed mood for most of day.
2. Disturbed appetite or change in weight.
3. Disturbed sleep.
4. Slow down in movement directly related to the brain or agitation
5. Loss of interest in previously pleasurable activities; inability to enjoy usual hobbies or activities
6. Fatigue or loss of energy
7. Feelings of worthlessness; excessive and/or inappropriate guilt
8. Difficulty concentrating or thinking clearly
9. Morbid or suicidal thoughts or actions

Depression Resources:
- National Depressive and Manic-Depressive Association: (800) 826-3632
- Depression and Related Affective Disorders Association: (410) 583-2919
- Recovery, Inc.: (312) 337-5661, www.recovery-inc.com
- 1-800-THERAPIST
- Depression: Awareness, Recognition & treatment (DART): (800) 421-4211

Body Image and Sexuality

We live in a culture that celebrates bodies. We see bodies all over—on billboards, television, magazines, newspapers—in various states of dress and undress. The type of body that is valued, however, is specific. In general, thin women with large breasts and tall men with big biceps and six pack abs are the celebrated images. Yet these body types are the exception among all human beings. As you know, bodies come in **all** shapes and sizes and very few people actually fit the mold of what society considers "perfect." In fact, the average female model weighs 23% less than the average woman, who weighs 144 pounds and wears between a size 12 and 14.

Body image concerns affect many people, both women and men, gay and straight, and across all races and ethnicities. The vast majority of people have at least one part of their body they don't like:

- *"My nose is too long."*
- *"I wish I had better abs."*
- *"I hate the flab on my thighs."*
- *"My breasts are too small."*
- *"I am not muscular enough."*

The diet industry encourages the focus on body "imperfections." Diet commercials are constantly appearing on our television screens telling us that once we lose the weight, we will be happy. The consequence? At least 80% of American women over the age of 18 are involved in some sort of dieting behavior and over 5 million Americans suffer from eating disorders.

Body image is directly related to sexuality. Many people have been raised to feel ashamed of their sexual body parts. Girls may have gotten the message that "down there" is dirty while boys learn to say words like "wee wee" and "pee pee" rather than "penis" in their families. In contrast, body parts such as female breasts are constantly objectified and celebrated in the media. These confusing and often conflicting messages can carry over into our sexual experiences. For example, wanting to have sex with the lights out or not wanting your partner to see you naked could be related to feelings of shame and embarrassment about your body.

It's normal to have a few body parts that you don't like or want to change. However, when the negative thoughts about your body take over and shape your entire opinion about yourself, interfere with your relationships, or lead to disordered eating, then body image and the behaviors in which you engage can become a problem.

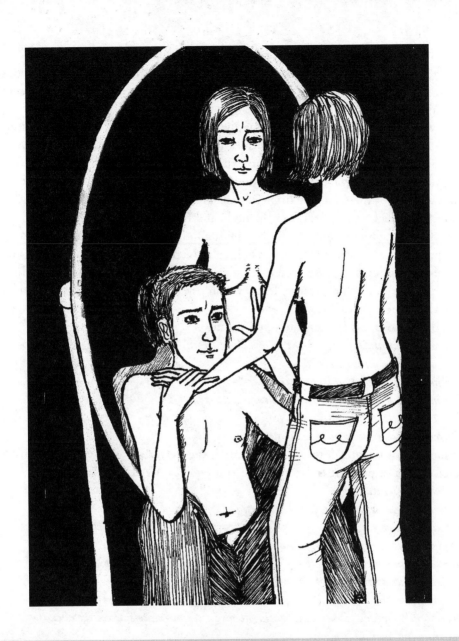

When Will She See Her Body the Way I Do?

My girlfriend is always asking me if I think she looks fat. She complains about her body and doesn't like to have sex with the lights on. I don't know what to do! I love her so much and think she is beautiful. I compliment her all the time and tell her she is hot. This is getting so frustrating, though, because I feel like she doesn't care what I think. Robert, 23 years old.

Anorexia nervosa is a serious, potentially life-threatening eating disorder characterized by self-starvation and excessive weight loss. Most (90-95%) people who suffer from anorexia nervosa are girls and women, making up about 1-2% of women in America. Anorexia nervosa is one of the most common psychiatric diagnoses in young women. Although anorexia primarily affects females, males are not immune. Despite the lack of studies on males with eating disorders, clinical reports suggest that about 1 out of 10 patients with anorexia or bulimia is male.

Because anorexia involves self-starvation, it can have very serious health consequences. Some of these include dry hair and skin, hair loss, or growth of a downy layer of hair called "lanugo" all over the body and face (in an effort to keep the body warm), fainting, fatigue, and overall weakness, abnormally slow heart rate and low blood pressure, increased risk for heart failure, reduction of bone density (osteoporosis), muscle loss and weakness, severe dehydration possibly leading to kidney failure. In severe cases, anorexia can cause death. Of all psychological disorders, anorexia has one of the highest death rates.

Anorexia nervosa has five primary symptoms:

1. *Refusal to maintain body weight at or above a minimally normal weight for height, body type, age, and activity level.*
2. *Intense fear of weight gain or being "fat."*
3. *Feeling "fat" or overweight despite dramatic weight loss.*
4. *Loss of menstrual periods in girls and women after puberty.*
5. *Extreme concern with body weight and shape.*

The sooner anorexia is detected and treated, the better the chances for recovery. Therefore, it's important to be aware of some of the WARNING SIGNS:

- *Dramatic weight loss.*
- *Preoccupation with weight, food, calories, fat grams, and dieting.*
- *Refusal to eat certain foods, progressing to restrictions against whole categories of food (i.e., no carbohydrates, etc.).*
- *Frequent comments about feeling "fat" or overweight despite weight loss.*
- *Anxiety about gaining weight or being "fat."*
- *Denial of hunger.*
- *Development of food rituals (i.e., eating foods in certain orders, excessive chewing, rearranging food on a plate).*
- *Consistent excuses to avoid mealtimes or situations involving food.*
- *Excessive, rigid exercise regimen—despite weather, fatigue, illness, or injury, the need to "burn off" calories taken in.*
- *Withdrawal from usual friends and activities.*
- *In general, behaviors and attitudes indicating that weight loss, dieting, and control of food are becoming primary concerns.*

Bulimia nervosa is a serious, potentially life-threatening eating disorder characterized by a cycles of binging (eating a lot of food) and purging (through self-induced vomiting, excessive exercise, fasting, or use of laxatives). Bulimia nervosa affects 1-3% of middle and high school girls and 1-4% of college age women. About 80% of people who have bulimia nervosa are female. Unlike anorexia nervosa, people with bulimia nervosa will often look like they are of average body weight.

Bulimia nervosa can cause harm to the body. The binge-and-purge cycles can affect the entire digestive system, leading to electrolyte and chemical imbalances in the body that affect the heart and other major organ functions. Other potential consequences include gastric rupture during periods of binging, inflammation and possible rupture of the esophagus from frequent vomiting, tooth decay and staining from stomach acids released during frequent vomiting. Chronic irregular bowel movements and constipation as a result of laxative abuse, and peptic ulcers and pancreatitis can also result.

Bulimia nervosa has three primary symptoms:

1. Eating large amounts of food in short periods of time (binging), often secretly, regardless of "hunger" or "fullness," and to the point of feeling "out of control" while eating.

2. Following binges, a person with bulimia will try to get rid of the food using a form of purging such as self-induced vomiting, laxative or diuretic abuse, fasting, and/or obsessive or compulsive exercise.

3. Extreme concern with body weight and shape.

The sooner bulimia is detected and treated, the better the chances for recovery. Therefore, it's important to be aware of some of the WARNING SIGNS:

- *Evidence of binge-eating, including disappearance of large amounts of food in short periods of time or the existence of wrappers and containers indicating the consumption of large amounts of food.*
- *Evidence of purging behaviors, including frequent trips to the bathroom after meals, signs and/or smells of vomiting, presence of wrappers or packages of laxatives or diuretics.*
- *Excessive, rigid exercise regimen—despite weather, fatigue, illness, or injury, the need to "burn off" calories taken in.*
- *Unusual swelling of the cheeks or jaw area.*
- *Calluses on the back of the hands and knuckles from self-induced vomiting.*
- *Discoloration or staining of the teeth.*
- *Creation of complex lifestyle schedules or rituals to make time for binge-and-purge sessions.*
- *Withdrawal from usual friends and activities.*
- *In general, behaviors and attitudes indicating that weight loss, dieting, and control of food are becoming primary concerns.*

*Source: Eating Disorders Awareness and Prevention, Inc.

Finding A Healthy Balance

In the end, it is important for every person to find a healthy balance when it comes to nutrition, body image, exercise, and self-esteem. This involves accepting that there are parts of you that you cannot change. It also involves changing what you can (e.g., eating a more nutritious diet, exercising more frequently, or seeking help if you have an eating disorder) in a healthy manner.

Purging Because of Sex

I just recovered from an eating disorder last year. I realized going through it that I had low self-esteem, but I never realized why. It seemed like I had a lot going for me, yet, looking back at my journal, I realized that every time I threw up, it was after I was with my boyfriend. I had sex to please him, even though I did not feel completely comfortable myself. It makes me sad... Diane, 20 years old.

Body Embarrassment

When I was in 6th grade and in a math class, one day I decided to take off my sweat shirt. I was in the front of the room and as I took off my sweatshirt, my t-shirt came off as well. I didn't really notice until the teacher asked me if I was about to strip. As I sat then with my revealing bird chest, the entire class burst out laughing. As if that wasn't bad enough for a young kid in puberty, the girls continued to harass me about it for the rest of the year. Kevin, 18 years old.

Have You Ever Really Thought About the Way You Talk to Your Body?

Many people think negative thoughts about their bodies. In fact, most people would never say the things they say about their bodies to another person. Can you imagine telling other people on a daily basis that they look fat, ugly, not good enough, or "if you could only lose 5 more pounds"? But how often do you say those things to yourself? A revealing activity is to put yourself in the shoes of the body part you criticize the most. How does it feel to be criticized in that way? What about all the good things this body part does for you? Would you talk to or treat another person this way? Why, then, is it OK to talk to yourself like this?

Next, practice saying some good things about your body. Compliment yourself. What are you good at physically? Maybe you are a fast runner, a good speaker, or are great at giving hugs? Maybe you've always gotten compliments about your hair, your nice smile, or your sexy eyes? Practice accepting these compliments from others as well as from yourself. Saying "thank you" without giving an excuse or disclaimer can go a long way in helping to increase self-esteem and positive body image.

*Adapted from: Transforming Body Image by M.G. Hutchinson.

Resources: Here are some resources you can use to find more information or get help on issues related to body image and eating disorders.
- Eating Disorders and Prevention, Inc.: (800) 931-2237 (toll-free information and referral hotline) www.edap.org
- Anorexia Nervosa and Related Eating Disorders, Inc.: www.anred.com
- Support, Concern, and Resources for Eating Disorders (S.C.a.R.E.D.): www.eating-disorder.org
- www.adiosbarbie.com: "a one-stop body shop, where women and men of all cultures and sizes can learn about their bodies and feel proud and comfortable in their natural shapes..."

Sexuality and Spirituality

People don't often think of sexuality and spirituality as related. As we emphasize throughout this book, people usually think of sexuality as only dealing with physical aspects—anatomy, physiology, and behavior. We have tried to demonstrate the important role psychology, emotions, communication, and relationships play in sexuality. But there can be a spiritual level to sexuality as well. For many people, sexuality encompasses a spritual component through the relationship one has with oneslf, with other people, or with a spiritual dimension or higher power. And, just as people conceptualize and experience sexuality in different ways, spiritual diversity is vast. From large religious institutions with centuries of history and teaching about sexuality to one person's unique connection with the universe and human energy, sexuality can be woven into many aspects of spirituality. For example, sexuality frequently involves intimacy, love, and connection, which are often important elements of spirituality.

Many religious institutions have established values and guidelines for sexuality, including specific sexual behaviors and sexual relationships with other people. Part of being a sexually healthy person is getting to know and accept your values, then making decisions that are in line with those values. For some people, this process may include acknowledging and embracing religious or spiritual values about sexuality. Whatever your spiritual values and beliefs are, it is important to recognize the role they play in your sexual identity and decision-making. When we are in touch with our values and beliefs, we can communicate them more effectively to friends, family members, and partners.

Masturbation

There is an old joke that says 95% of people masturbate and the other 5% of the population lies about it. Most people can't talk about masturbation, much less say the word, but most people do masturbate. Why do people have so many hang-ups when it comes to pleasuring ourselves? From a very early age many people are taught that touching themselves is bad, dirty, or wrong. These messages often contribute to feelings of guilt or shame when masturbating. However, there are many positives about masturbation. For instance, it can help people know their bodies better, which may result in a more satisfying sex life individually and/or with a partner.

What is masturbation? Masturbation is self-stimulation of the genitals or other body parts. Typically, people masturbate for pleasure—because it feels good—but there are many other possible reasons, including relaxation, stress relief, fun, to help get to sleep, or to share the experience with a partner.

People may choose to masturbate in different ways. For some it may be a slow, drawn-out process, involving all of the senses such as touch, smell, sound, and sight. Some people may like to play music or light a scented candle or incense while others may like to fantasize while they stimulate themselves. Others prefer to focus just on "getting off." Some people prefer lubrication such as Astroglide, Eros, Wet, hand lotion, saliva, or soapsuds when masturbating as a way of increasing the sensitivity, whereas others may not use any lubrication.

You may be curious just how people masturbate. Some women use their fingers or hand to rub the clitoris or may insert their fingers into their vagina or anus. They may use a vibrator or dildo for stimulation. Some men may use the technique of circling their hand around the shaft of the penis and stroking it in an up and down or back and forth motion. They may also choose to touch the scrotum and testicles or insert a finger or object into the anus. While masturbating, both men and women may stimulate body parts other than their genitals such as the breasts, nipples, inner thighs, lips, or hair. Remember, there is no "right" or "wrong" way to masturbate—it's whatever feels best to you.

Many people also fantasize while masturbating. An important concept to remember is that your mind and your fantasies are the ultimate turn-on. There are no bad fantasies. Just because you fantasize about something does not mean you will act it out or that you want it to happen.

Some people may choose not to masturbate. This is okay, too. The bottom line is that masturbation will not harm you in any way—that's right, all those stories about growing hair on your hands, going blind, or men running out of sperm are myths. And, yes, people in long-term relationships often continue to masturbate. This can be important time spent with yourself or shared with a partner. Whether you choose to masturbate or not, know that it is a healthy and common human behavior.

Resources: For more information about masturbation, check out:
- www.sexetc.org
- www.positive.org
- www.BettyDodson.com
- www.jackinworld.com

Masturbation Makes My Partner Uncomfortable

Even though I am sexually active with my girlfriend of one year, I still masturbate often. After having sex with her, I will go home and "jack off" 95% of the time. We only see each other about twice a week and I have told her that I do this. I think it is a healthy way of satisfying my sexual desire. I enjoy the ejaculation more (when masturbating) because I'm a little more in control and I have a great imagination. I think I have sex to please my girlfriend and masturbate to please myself. My girlfriend does not like this because she feels it's her job to make me happy, and she does a good job at it. She does not understand why I continue to do it because she never has. Samuel, 24 years old.

Proud to Admit It!
I'm a 20-year-old female and I'm proud to say that I masturbate. My friends think I'm crazy to even talk about it but I feel like it shows I'm in touch with myself and my body. I'm not planning on having sex until I get in a very committed relationship and masturbation helps me deal with my sexual desire, especially when I fantasize while doing it. I think a lot of women feel the way I do about masturbation, but maybe are afraid to admit it. Kelly, 20 years old.

A Pleasurable Experience
I am not afraid to admit I masturbate. I personally think everyone masturbates. I enjoy it. It satisfies my incredible urges. Plus, my partner loves to watch me masturbate and I love to watch her. It's a mainstay in our sexual repetoire. Andrew, 22 years old.

Am I Normal?

Most people's questions about sexuality center on concerns about normalcy. Just having the word "normal" implies that there is an "abnormal," so it's no surprise that people are curious. Moreover, because sexuality is not generally talked about openly, people are left wondering if their bodies, behaviors, and feelings are "normal." These questions are difficult to answer because there is not one, clear definition for the word normal. While some people use a statistical definition—the proportion of people who have, believe, or do something—others base their ideas of normalcy on moral or ethical standards.

However, because statistics only reflect prevalence and moral and ethical standards run into the problem of relativism (what's normal for you may not be normal for me), these definitions can be problematic. Better criteria for evaluating sexual behaviors and attitudes might involve asking the following questions:

• *Is the situation/condition/behavior causing me harm or interfering with my life and relationships?*
• *Is the situation/condition/behavior in line with my values?*
• *Is the situation/condition/behavior causing harm to others?*
• *Is the situation/condition/behavior mutually consensual?*

Even these questions can get tricky to answer when it comes to sexuality. For instance, a person who doesn't feel very good about him or herself may not realize that having sex while drunk is harming them. Or, a person may be confused about his or her values about having sex before marriage or while still in college. In the end, it is important to sit down and think seriously about these questions before making sexual decisions.

Communication Tip:

Remember, it's *normal* to wonder if you are "normal" sexually! Use this book to help find reassurance and answers. It may also be helpful to talk to trusted friends or relatives. Sometimes just finding out that you are not the "only" one with a particular question or concern can make you feel better.

Am I Abnormal?

I have never masturbated before. I just feel uncomfortable playing with myself. It does not satisfy me to the point where I can have an orgasm. My friends did not believe me when I said I never masturbate. Am I abnormal? Jared, 17 years old.

Orgasm and Sexual Response

Many people have questions about orgasms. The Big "O" is mysterious to young and old alike. What is an orgasm and how does it feel? How does it happen? How can I experience one (or more)? To understand an orgasm, one must understand that the brain is the body's most powerful sexual organ. The mind dictates many of the forces that "create" an orgasm. Without the mental and psychological processes generated by the mind such as fantasy, excitement, pleasure, and relaxation, an orgasm is unlikely. In addition, the brain releases chemicals (called *oxytocin*) that are involved in the experience of orgasm. Involving anatomy is important, but an orgasm really could be described as being "all in your head!"

Several prominent researchers have dedicated their lives to understanding orgasm and sexual response. Along with the mental and psychological processes involved in an orgasm, there are physical changes that often occur simultaneously with what happens in the mind. Some people describe an orgasm as similar to a sneeze that builds and builds until finally the sneeze occurs and it feels as if there has been a big release. Physiologically, there is a build up of pressure (called *vasocongestion)*, which involves the in-flow of blood into the genitals. Along with vasocongestion, the muscles in the body contract (called *myotonia*) and then release during orgasm, producing the sensation of a "release."

The following description of the sexual response cycle elaborates upon the stages a person goes through before, during, and after orgasm. The four stages below are derived from the work of several prominent sex researchers and therapists, including William Masters, Virginia Johnson, Helen Singer Kaplan, and David Reed. We combine these researchers' ideas on the sexual response cycle to help illustrate the simultaneous physical and mental processes that occur. This information, through increasing an understanding of the flow of events, may help a person experience orgasm. It is also important to note that any of these "stages" in the sexual response cycle can be an end in and of itself. In other words, orgasm does not have to be the "goal" of all sexual activity.

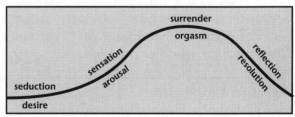

SEXUAL RESPONSE CYCLE

1. *Seduction,* also called the *desire* phase, is when the mind and body first become sexually stimulated. Erotic thoughts, attractions, turn-ons, rituals, and anxieties may be a catalyst for desire. This stage is important because without the triggers of seduction, the sexual response cycle would not begin. Because many people have been conditioned to turn-off their sexual desires and do not give themselves permission to feel sexual, it is at this stage that people most frequently experience sexual dysfunction.

2. *Sensation,* also called the *arousal* phase, is the process through which the body and mind experience further increased sexual arousal. Blood flows into the genitals causing the penis to get erect, the vulva to swell slightly, and the vagina to lubricate. Heart rate, breathing, and muscular tension increase. Touching and caressing feel more intense when a person is aroused. These processes continue until they reach a point at which no more arousal is possible, also called *plateau.*

3. *Surrender,* also called *orgasm,* is when a person allows him or herself to "let go," "be in the moment," and "surrender control." During orgasm, the muscles in and around the genitals contract and release at approximately 0.8-second intervals and the muscles of the body contract and then release. Blood flows rapidly out of the genitals, creating feelings of intense pleasure in waves throughout the body. In men, these contractions cause semen to be ejaculated out of the urethra. (It is important to note that ejaculation and orgasm are not the same and do not have to occur simultaneously, although they usually do). Some women also ejaculate fluid from the urethra, usually after vaginal stimulation in an area called the Grafenberg, or "G," spot (see page 6). Current research indicates that this fluid is not urine and does not come from the bladder. Rather, experts believe the fluid is similar chemically to the fluid produced by the prostate in the male and is believed to come from the Skene's glands. People who are unable to surrender control, be vulnerable, or let the body "release" may have problems experiencing orgasm.

4. *Reflection,* also called *resolution,* is the period following orgasm where the muscles of the body relax and blood flows out of the genitals. It is also during this post-orgasm state that the individual may reflect upon the previous events. The period after orgasm when most males need to wait to become aroused again is called the *refractory* period. Age, health, genetics, and resiliency will determine how fast the penis may become erect following orgasm. Some males do not lose their erection after orgasm and can remain erect for multiple orgasms. While some females also experience a sort of refractory period, others can have multiple orgasms, one right after another.

Communication Tip:
One of the best ways to be able to explain to your partner what feels good to you and how you like to experience pleasure is to practice on yourself! Self-pleasuring and self-exploration can help you better understand what is pleasurable for you so that you can explain your technique, fantasies, or positions to your partner.

SEXUAL DIFFICULTIES AND DYSFUNCTION

Healthy sexual functioning is an important part of your overall health. We have included this brief guide to help you become aware of different sexual problems. If you think one of the descriptions applies to you or your partner, we recommend discussing the issue with your health care provider or a sex counselor or therapist. Most sexual problems can be treated with the help of qualified professionals. To get the number of a certified sex therapist or counselor in your area, go to the American Association of Sex Educators, Counselors, and Therapists (AASECT) website: www.aasect.org/directory. Many colleges and universities also have trained sex counselors to provide this service at low or no cost to students. Check with your student health center for more information.

Female Sexual Dysfunction

Decreased Sexual Desire

• *What is it?* Decreased sexual desire is when a woman has no or a very low sex drive. This lack of desire is a sexual dysfunction when it causes problems for her personally and in her sexual relationship(s). Decreased desire is relative to original levels of desire or to a partner's desire. There is no absolute "normal" level. This is a very common problem—about 1 out of every 3 women has a lack of desire for some period of time during her life.

• *What causes it?* The cause is frequently psychologically-related. Things like relationship problems or stress from school or work might cause a woman to have less sexual desire. In addition, having been sexually abused in the past, or using alcohol and other drugs can decrease her sexual desire. Decreased desire also can be related to medical problems such as depression, a hormone imbalance, and other disorders. For example, having a low level of testosterone may lead to decreased sex drive. Sometimes a woman may have less desire after she starts using a hormonal contraceptive such as birth control pills.

• *How is it treated?* A woman may need to be examined by a medical doctor and/or speak with a counselor. If a medical problem is causing the lack of desire, treatment of that problem may help increase desire. Sometimes the hormone testosterone is given to increase sex drive. If there are psychological reasons, she and her partner (if she has one) can work with a counselor or therapist to treat the problem. NOTE: If the woman is in a relationship, this is usually not "just her problem." It is important that both partners are involved in the treatment. When there is a problem in a relationship, both partners play a role in the problem and the solution. In a couple, it's rarely one person's fault.

Excessive Sexual Desire

• *What is it?* Excessive sexual desire is when a woman has sexual desire that is out of her control. It may lead her to act in obsessive-compulsive ways. She may act out her desire in ways that are directly harmful to herself and others (unprotected sex with many partners, perpetrating sexual abuse).

• *What causes it?* The causes are complicated. They are usually psychological, related in some way to a woman's past experience. For example, she may have been sexually abused as a child and is acting out what she learned while growing up. Low self-esteem and depression may also be related. Drug or alcohol use can complicate the problem.

• *How is it treated?* Treatment varies depending on the type and cause. Individual and group therapy are usually used. Therapeutic techniques used to treat obsessive-compulsive behaviors are often helpful.

Anorgasmia: Primary

• *What is it?* Primary anorgasmia is when a woman has never had an orgasm—neither while masturbating nor during sexual activity with a partner—and wishes to have an orgasm.

• *What causes it?* The cause is usually psychological. Some women may not know how their bodies and sexual response cycles work. Others may have performance anxiety—they are so focused on reaching the goal of orgasm (performing) that the anxiety stops them from relaxing enough to do so. Other women may have been taught that sex is bad, or have been abused, which stops them from being able to relax and enjoy sex.

• *How is it treated?* Depending on the cause, it is usually treated by seeing a counselor or therapist. There are exercises a couple can do to help decrease the pressure to perform during sex. These are called *sensate focus* exercises, during which the woman tries to focus on *all* of her sexual feelings without trying to achieve the "goal" of orgasm. Getting to know her body through self-pleasuring may also help her identify what feels good to her. If a woman is in a relationship, anorgasmia may affect the relationship. Therefore, a counselor will most likely want to work with the woman and her partner together.

Never Had An Orgasm

I'm a 20-year-old woman and I've never had an orgasm, or at least I don't think so. I've had two sex partners in the past and even though I enjoyed being with them, didn't climax. I masturbate on occasion but always seem to stop before anything resembling orgasm (or what I think it would feel like) happens. Jessica, 20 years old.

Anorgasmia: Secondary or Situational

• *What is it?* Secondary, or situational, anorgasmia is when a woman has had orgasms in the past—either while masturbating or during sexual activity with a partner—but is unable to presently or in certain situations.

• *What causes it?* The cause is usually psychological or situational. For example, a woman may be able to experience orgasm when she masturbates, but not when she is with her partner. (NOTE: If she is able to orgasm during oral sex or mutual masturbation with a partner, but not during intercourse, this does not necessarily mean that she has anorgasmia. *Most* women do not orgasm from penile thrusting alone—stimulation of the clitoris is needed). Other reasons may be having a new partner or having performance anxiety. Medical problems such as neurological (brain, spinal cord, nerves) or vascular (heart, blood vessels) diseases may also underlie anorgasmia. Medicines for depression, blood pressure, and other problems can significantly diminish both sex drive and the ability to have orgasms.

• *How is it treated?* Similar treatments are used with secondary anorgasmia as with primary anorgasmia (see above).

Vaginismus

• *What is it?* Vaginismus involves painful, spastic contractions (like cramps) of the pelvic muscles that happens upon attempted insertion of a penis, finger, or other object into the vagina.

• *What causes it?* The cause is usually psychological. A woman may have been sexually abused, may be having sex when she does not want to, or may have been taught that sex is bad or negative. Vaginismus also can happen when sex is painful due to infection, scarring, or a very small opening of the vagina. Future contractions are then an unconscious response to protect the woman from further pain. NOTE: Sometimes it is difficult to tell the difference between vaginismus and dyspareunia (painful intercourse). It is important to see a qualified health care provider in order to get a correct diagnosis and treatment.

• *How is it treated?* It is usually treated using an exercise in which a woman (alone or with her partner) slowly works on relaxing her vagina by inserting progressively larger dilators while consciously relaxing the vaginal muscles.

Dyspareunia

• *What is it?* Dyspareunia is when a woman experiences pain when a penis, finger, or other object is inserted into the vagina.

• *What causes it?* The cause is often related to a medical problem such as a urinary tract infection, a sexually transmitted infection, endometriosis, pelvic inflammatory disease, fibroids, interstitial cystitis, or spinal column disc diseases. Dryness of the vaginal lining or a sexually transmitted infection also may cause pain. In addition, dyspareunia can be related to psychological factors such as having been sexually abused, taught that sex is bad, or being in an unhappy relationship.

• *How is it treated?* It is important to see a qualified health care provider in order to get a correct diagnosis and treatment. Some medical problems, such as infections, can be treated to help relieve the pain. Dryness in the vagina can be treated easily using a lubricant such as Astroglide, Eros, or K-Y Jelly. Other medical problems are more difficult to treat and may require the woman and her partner to find sexual positions and activities that are less painful. Seeing a counselor or therapist may be necessary to treat psychological causes and/or to help a woman and her partner (if she has one) work through the psychological effects of dyspareunia.

Male Sexual Dysfunction

Decreased Sexual Desire

• *What is it?* Decreased sexual desire is when a man has no or a very low sex drive. This lack of desire is a sexual dysfunction when it causes problems for him personally and in his sexual relationship(s). Decreased desire is relative to previous levels of desire or to a partner's desire. There is no absolute "normal" level.

• *What causes it?* The cause is often psychological. Things like relationship problems or family, financial, career, or school stress might cause a man to have less sexual desire. In addition, having been sexually abused in the past and using drugs and alcohol can decrease his sexual desire. It also can be related to medical problems such as certain diseases, depression, and a hormone imbalance. For example, a low level of testosterone may lead to decreased sex drive.

• *How is it treated?* A man may need to be examined by a medical doctor and a psychologist. If a medical problem is causing him to have a lack of desire, treatment can start with that problem. If there are psychological reasons, he and his partner (if he has one) can work with a counselor or therapist to treat the problem. NOTE: If the man is in a relationship, this is not usually "just his problem." It is important that both partners are involved in the treatment. Both partners are affected when one has a lack of sexual desire.

Excessive Sexual Desire

• *What is it?* Excessive sexual desire is when a man has sexual desire that is out of his control. It may lead him to act in obsessive-compulsive ways. He may act out his desire in ways that are directly harmful to others (rape, child sexual abuse, publicly exposing himself, or making obscene phone calls).

• *What causes it?* The causes are complicated. They are usually psychological, related in some way to a man's past experience. For example, he may have been sexually abused as a child and is acting out what he learned while growing up. Drugs or alcohol frequently complicate the problem.

• *How is it treated?* Treatment varies depending on the type and cause. Therapeutic techniques used to treat obsessive-compulsive behaviors are often helpful. In some cases, a man is jailed for offenses such as rape, incest, and child abuse and will also go through intensive group and individual therapy. Medicines such as Depo-Provera also are used to help reduce excessive and out-of-control sexual desire.

Early Ejaculation

• *What is it?* Early ejaculation, also called "premature" ejaculation, is when a man ejaculates (comes) without any voluntary control. It is difficult to say how early is "too" early. One definition is ejaculation in less than a minute of penile thrusting during sexual intercourse. However, because this can vary greatly for each person, sex therapists often base the diagnosis on the man's subjective evaluation of his and his partner's pleasure and satisfaction rather than on a specific length of time. Early ejaculation is more common among young men.

• *What causes it?* The cause is usually psychological. Early ejaculation is often a learned behavior, which means that a man has formed a "habit" based on his past behavior. For example, boys often learn to masturbate in a setting where they are in a hurry, perhaps trying not to get caught. This habit then may carry over into his sexual behavior with a partner. Rarely, it may also be related to neurological (brain, spinal cord, nerves) diseases such as multiple sclerosis and possibly infections such as urethritis.

• *How is it treated?* A man and his partner may work with a counselor to "unlearn" the behavior. Two techniques are commonly used—the "start-stop" technique and the "squeeze" technique. In the "start-stop" technique, the man tells his partner when he is just about to ejaculate. His partner stops stimulating the penis for 30 seconds, then starts again. In the "squeeze" technique, the man tells his partner when he is just about to ejaculate. His partner gently squeezes the glans, or head, of the penis for 4-5 seconds. Both techniques can be repeated during sexual activity until the man feels he has more control over his ejaculation. Finally, using condoms or taking small doses of the anti-depressant Prozac also can help treat early ejaculation.

Came Really Quickly
One time I was having oral sex with this girl. After she started, I came in thirty seconds. I was really embarrassed because we were planning to have sex afterwards, but I could not, at least not for a while. Cole, 20 years old.

Delayed Ejaculation

• *What is it?* Delayed ejaculation, also called "retarded" ejaculation, is when a man is unable to or has problems having an orgasm during sexual activity with a partner.

• *What causes it?* Similar to early ejaculation, the cause is often psychological and may reflect a learned behavior. For example, a man may masturbate in a way that allows him to orgasm. When he cannot repeat this pattern with a partner, he may have trouble experiencing orgasm. It also may happen if a man has performance anxiety; that is, he feels so much pressure to orgasm that it gets in the way of him doing so. Finally, it is important that a man get checked by a health care provider to make sure that medical problems are not the cause.

• *How is it treated?* Some sex therapists use what is called a "demand" strategy, in which a man's partner stimulates his penis manually and switches to intercourse just as he is about to orgasm. Others prefer to treat delayed ejaculation similar to anorgasmia in a woman. In this method, called "sensate focus," a couple tries to reduce the pressure to ejaculate by having the man focus on *all* sexual feelings rather than focusing only on the "goal" of orgasm.

Erectile Dysfunction: Primary

Primary erectile dysfunction (ED) is when a man has never been able to get an erection and have sexual intercourse. This is an uncommon problem that usually occurs when a man has high levels of anxiety about sexual performance. It is a good idea for a man to have medical and psychological exams to determine the cause and best treatment.

Erectile Dysfunction: Secondary

• *What is it?* Secondary erectile dysfunction (ED) is when a man has been able to get erections in the past and cannot currently, or can get an erection in some situations (e.g., masturbation) but not in others (e.g., with a partner). This is a common problem. About 30 million men in the U.S. have ED, and half of those are under age 65. Although the prevalence of secondary ED increases with age, it can also occur in younger men as a result of cigarette smoking, use of alcohol and other drugs, and as a side effect of certain medications.

• *What causes it?* In the past, it was thought that ED was "all in a man's head." But we now know that approximately 85% of men with ED have a physical cause for the problem. Diabetes is the most common cause. Other causes include heart disease, spinal cord injury, using alcohol, cigarettes, and other drugs, and taking certain prescription medicines such as antidepressants.

• *How is it treated?* A man needs to have a medical exam to determine the cause. If it is physical, there are many medical treatments available, including Viagra, vacuum devices, injection therapy, urethral inserts, implants, and surgery. Counseling may be necessary for 28 psychological causes or if ED has caused problems in a man's relationships.

No Sexual Desire

I'm a sophomore and very distressed. Not only do I choose to abstain from sex, but I have never dated, kissed a girl, or have had any desire to do anything sexually. I'm sad because I know my feelings aren't normal. My best friend, Jake, is the first person I've ever told about this. I'm happy being single, but wonder why I have such a nonexistent libido. Drew, 19 years old.

SELF EXAMS

Touching your body not only can be pleasurable, it also can be an important investment in your health and wellness. You must know what your body usually looks, feels, smells, and tastes like to notice any changes that are "out-of-the-usual." For instance, if you do not know your own body, how can you notice a growth or a mole that has changed color? Doing self-exams can help you get to know yourself. Exams are intended to help you notice any suspicious changes, growths, or other characteristics that are not "normal" for you and your body.

Partners can help one another examine their bodies. It can be fun to do things with your partner that contribute to your health! However, it is important that you do not rely on your partner to take responsibility for your health. Whether alone, or with a partner, regular exams are a fundamental part of self-care.

Self Testicular Examination:

Testicular cancer is the most common cancer in young men between the ages of 15 and 35 years old— but any man, at any age, can get testicular cancer. It is important for young men to get in the habit of checking their testicles for irregular lumps once a month starting at puberty and continuing throughout the lifespan. The earlier any irregularity is noticed, the earlier it can be brought to the attention of a health care professional and the better chance for early diagnosis and treatment. The exam should be done during or after a hot shower or bath. The warmth of the water generally causes the scrotum (the sac that contains the testicles) to relax making it easier to feel and find any irregularities.

• *Step One:* Gently examine each individual testicle by feeling and rolling it with your fingers and thumb, checking for any lump or irregularity.

• *Step Two:* Make sure not to confuse the epididymis for a lump or growth. The epididymis is located on the top of each testicle and stores mature sperm. If a lump is found, it usually will be about the size of a pea and will be located on the front or side of the testicle. If any small growth(s) is found, if you feel discomfort in your testicle, or if fluid accumulates in your scrotum, see your health care provider immediately.

• *Step Three:* After your shower and testicular examination, stand naked in front of a mirror and look for any unusual changes on your body.

[Adapted from: Hyde, J. & DeLamater, J. (1997). Understanding Human Sexuality, 6th Edition. New York: McGraw-Hill.]

Resources: For more information and resources on testicular cancer, see:
• The Testicular Cancer Resource Center: www.acor.org/diseases/TC
• American Cancer Society: www3.cancer.org or 1-800-ACS-2345
• Lance Armstrong Foundation: www.laf.org

Self Breast Examination:

Due to increased awareness of breast examinations, more women are discovering, treating, and surviving breast cancer than ever before. if detected early, breast cancer is one of the most treatable forms of cancer! It is important for young women to get in the habit of checking their breasts for irregular lumps once a month starting at puberty and continuing throughout the lifespan. The earlier any irregularity is noticed, the earlier it can be brought to the attention of a health care professional and the better chance for early diagnosis and treatment.

• *Step One - In the Shower:* Your hands will glide more easily over a wet and soapy body. With the pads of your index, middle, and ring fingers held flat, move them gently over each part of the breast. Starting at the outermost top edge, move your fingers in a circular motion towards the nipple. Use the right hand to examine your left breast (with your left arm raised holding the back of your neck) and your left hand to examine your right breast (with your right arm raised holding the back of your neck). Examine each breast in this manner twice - once with light pressure and once with deep pressure. You will be checking for any hard lump, knot, dimpling, thickening, or anything different from previous exams. Do your exam on the same day each month, 7-10 days after your period has begun.

• *Step Two - In Front of a Mirror:* Try to notice any changes with your breasts or body while you are in various positions: arms over your head, arms at your sides, hand clasped under your chin while flexing your chest muscles, and bent over leaning forward. Regular examinations will tell you what is "normal" for you and your body.

• *Step Three - Lying Down:* Place a small folded towel or a small pillow under your back on the side that you are examining. Rub lotion on your breast and repeat the finger pad examination in a circular motion from the outside inward towards the nipple (from 12 o'clock to 1 o'clock and so forth until back to 12). A small ridge of firm tissue in the lower curve of each breast is to be expected. While examining the right breast place your right hand behind your head, which should distribute your breast tissue more evenly on your chest. Finally, squeeze the nipple of each breast gently. If you notice any clear or bloody discharge you should bring your observation to the attention of a health care professional immediately.

• *Mammography:* Women should have a mammogram at 40 years of age and every other year thereafter until they turn 50. At the age of 50, women should have a mammogram annually.

NOTE: Guys can do self breast exams, too. Men have breasts - even if they prefer to call them "pecs." Men can and do get breast cancer (an estimated 1500 men will be diagnosed every year), so it is worth performing regular exams.

[Adapted from: Hyde, J & DeLamater, J. (1997). <u>Understanding Human Sexuality, 6th Edition.</u> New York: McGraw-Hill.]

Resources: For more information and resources on breast cancer, see:
• American Cancer Society Breast Cancer Network:
  www2.cancer.org/bcn/index.html or 1-800-ACS-2345
• Susan G. Komen Breast Cancer Foundation: www.komen.org or
  www.breastcancerinfo.com

CHAPTER 3:
Relationships With Others

There is probably nothing more complex yet rewarding than a quality relationship. Conversely, there is probably nothing more painful than a bad relationship. Relationships take hard work to nurture and maintain. It is a myth that if you hold out long enough for the right person you will find him or her, and then your relationship will be easy and free of disagreements and problems. That relationship exists only in fairy tales because it is fictitious! However, if a relationship becomes nothing but pain, disappointment, and problems, it is probably beneficial to find a more fulfilling and satisfying one. Figuring out when to hold onto a relationship and when to concede or let go is a difficult challenge. Hopefully, this book will provide valuable insight into when to stay, when to go, or when it is worthwhile to put in some work, and what that work may involve.

There are many forms of relationships. There are friendships, family members, acquaintances, teachers, sports teams, lovers, partners, husbands, wives, and so forth. Sometimes individuals enjoy relationships with their same gender, with a different gender, or with both genders. There is not one "best" type of relationship. It is not the label on the relationship that makes a relationship "healthy" or "moral;" it is how the individuals in the relationship treat one another. Regardless of the form your relationship takes, it will most likely need some of the same general investments such as communication, flexibility, understanding, forgiveness, caring, and hard work.

The bottom line on relationships is that they should be defined by the people involved in them. What is okay in one friendship may not be okay in another. What is acceptable in one marriage may not be acceptable in another. As long as the people in the relationship are consenting and are not violating anyone's rights, they should have the ability to make their relationships suit their needs. We are each unique and should be respected for how we live our relationships.

Communication

Communication is monumentally important in all forms of relationships. Unfortunately, we are not all innately good communicators. Communication takes practice. Our culture tells us various messages about who is "allowed" to express certain feelings, thoughts, or values and when we are "allowed" to express them. Those who cannot communicate their feelings, needs, desires, pain, or joy are sadly lacking the ability to express themselves and their needs to their friends, family, and fellow human beings. Lacking such skills sometimes results in those feelings "leaking out" in various forms. Sometimes the external expression of our internal feelings through art, poetry, or sports can be positive. Other times the way people express their emotions, such as violence and harming oneself, can be negative and destructive. Human beings find ways, sometimes healthy and sometimes unhealthy, of conveying to the world what is going on with their feelings. Being able to communicate verbally is a way of getting our needs met and letting the world know who we are and what we are feeling.

There is no doubt that communication, especially about sexuality, can be difficult and many times uncomfortable or awkward. For many people, communicating about such issues as sexual behaviors, intimacy, feelings, experiences with previous partners, drug use, sickness, contraception, or how we like to be pleasured can be anxiety producing. In our culture, where sex is usually only joked about or not talked about at all, it is totally natural to feel awkward or embarrassed. With some practice, however, communicating about sexuality, relationships, feelings, and such topics can become much more comfortable to explore.

As difficult as communicating about some of these issues may seem, they are fairly easy when compared with getting pregnant, not having an orgasm, keeping silent about a date rape experience, or getting infected with a sexually transmitted infection and having to tell your future sex partners. Sometimes we must jump difficult small hurdles so that we do not end up at the incredibly difficult large hurdles. If you like someone enough to share their body, perhaps you should at a minimum be able to speak with that person about sex beforehand. If you know that you absolutely cannot communicate about contraception, sexual histories, or feelings, you may not be ready to engage in such behaviors with that particular person. Please, remember - if your partner won't talk about or bring up safer sexual practices they probably haven't with other partners as well. If your partner doesn't insist upon protection with you, he or she probably hasn't insisted on it with others. It is your health and well being on the line— it is worth it to communicate!

Dishonest About Her Sexual History

When I was 17 years old, I had unprotected sex with a female who claimed to be a virgin. I used the withdrawal technique. Later, I found out that she had been sexually active for about a year. That scared me for a long while. I went and got a blood test later that week and then the next year. The experience changed my life, and I often wonder how things would be different if we had only talked more and gotten to know each other better beforehand. Angel, 20 years old.

Relationships with others always involve agreement and disagreement. How the individuals in the relationship handle their disagreements will powerfully affect the closeness and overall "flavor" of the relationship. When people get together it is almost as if two different cultures were coming together. We each contain perspectives and opinions about family, politics, sexuality, religion, spirituality, child-rearing, pets, nutrition, and so forth. Those that anticipate, prepare for, and embrace differences may be at an advantage over those who do not allow for differences of opinion within relationships.

Communication is an ongoing process that should allow for growth and changing attitudes and values. What people believe and value one day may not necessarily be what is important to them six months later. Thus, it is important for people in relationships to check-in with and keep getting to know one another.

One of the most important things about communication is that it can be fun! With practice and a willing partner, communication can be improved, learned, and celebrated. It is a worthy investment if you can make communication a strong presence in your relationship.

Communication Tip #1:

When communicating, there is a major difference between a dialogue and a debate. Debate should be left in the courtroom or for the "Debate Club" at school. Debate is about winning and losing a conversation! Even the "winner" of a conversation often feels poorly after communicating. Who enjoys seeing their friends and loved ones lose or have their beliefs dismissed? If every conversation becomes a battle or a win-lose situation the communication will not be fun and will no doubt be avoided at all costs. Dialogue is about expressing where you are at and what thoughts and experiences have gotten you to such a place. Debate tries to disprove or destroy ideas, thoughts, and feelings. Dialogue tries to explore different perspectives and find the common ground in different peoples' ideas and discover the most mutually beneficial arrangement as possible.

Communication Tip #2:

Sometimes in a relationship, it is difficult to tell exactly when a partner is joking or when they are serious. Too much room for interpretation can cause miscommunication, anger, and unnecessary pain. One method partners or friends in a relationship can use to identify when they are absolutely serious is to select a "codeword." This word must be held sacred by everyone involved. When this word is used, it is the final call. It is a "stop" button. Whether the situation is sexual, tickling, inappropriate teasing, or telling a story at dinner that you would prefer not be brought up, your codeword can help you and your partner better understand one another's boundaries. Another benefit of developing a codeword is that your particular word can be used without anyone else knowing that you are telling your partner that you are serious and to stop. Whereas "quit it" or "please stop" can sometimes be interpreted differently depending upon the tone of voice and the situation, a mutually agreed upon codeword can stop the action and explicitly illustrate your boundary.

Honesty Helped Us Stay Together

My current relationship with my boyfriend is the best I've ever had. We have really worked at being honest with each other, which wasn't always easy. There were times when we thought it was over, but we hung in there and worked through stuff. I'll always think of him as my best friend. Jordan, 24 years old.

Why Are We Always Arguing?

My boyfriend and I are always fighting. We have been together for 3 years and it seemed like the perfect relationship the first 2 years. Then something changed. We are always at each other's throats now. I swear he doesn't hear one word I say! It's like we just go back and forth over the same issues, never resolving any of our differences. Brie, 23 years old.

"Hooking-Up"

Hooking-up is a frequently used term that can have many different meanings. To some people it means intercourse while to others it means kissing. It may be valuable to explore and identify what hooking-up means to your friends and dates.

Everyone chooses to express themselves physically in different ways. Some people kiss, some cuddle, some have intercourse. Some people feel the need to be emotionally close before being physical while others do not. Some people believe pleasure is an acceptable motivation for being physical, others do not. There is no right way or one correct set of values – as long as everyone involved is consenting.

Sometimes people feel awkward the day after a hook-up. There are many messages in the media that say friends cannot hook-up and that somehow sex has the capacity to destroy relationships between friends. If you are concerned that the day after a hook-up you may feel uncomfortable or may lose your friend, it would be beneficial to share those feelings or concerns. Being physical with someone else is an individual decision that we all must make for ourselves. It only has the power and meaning that we give it. If you believe that being physical will destroy the relationship or that you and your partner don't have the communication skills to manage a "hook-up," perhaps your beliefs will be self-fulfilling. Conversely, if you believe that being physical would be fun and that you and your partner or friend could maintain communication about needs, wants, desires, and what life will be like after the hook-up, it may be the result you get.

Communication Tip:

Honesty about expectations and desires begins with you! It may take courage to admit to yourself that you want something. However, it may be best to explain what you want to a partner up front. Sometimes people are taught that it is better to lie to someone to get what you want. Overall, most people would rather be told the truth than be lied to with lines such as "I love you - do you want to go upstairs?" If you are honest, with yourself and partner, everyone can enter the situation knowing the true intentions and motivations of their partner.

We Hooked Up and Stayed Close Friends

I was friends with two beautiful women. I had deep feelings for both of them. One night we all went out to dinner and then went back to my place. One thing led to another and we all started hooking up. It was incredibly hot but the most important thing that I took away from the experience was that I cared deeply for both of these people and they cared about me. Of course it was incredible in the physical sense, but it was also wonderful emotionally. Afterwards, we all remained close and it did not harm our friendship— in fact, made us closer. Carlos, 26 years old.

Dating

There may be nothing more exciting than going out on a date—the anticipation of making a new friend, being accepted and appreciated, and the fear of being rejected all rolled into one moment.

Many people think of dating as a rehearsal for a long-term partnership or marriage. But what if dating and spending time with people you care about has value in and of itself? You don't have to date only to interview marriage candidates. Some people choose only to date possible long-term or marriage partners and that is fine, too. In general, dating can and should be a fun way to socialize and get to know people.

Communication Tip:

In this day and age, think about including the following in a hot first date—going to buy condoms, taking your partner's sexual history, or getting tested for sexually transmitted infections. Thse activities may not seem like much fun, but they are crucial to your and your partner's sexual health and can increase the honesty and intimacy in your new relationship. It's good to set healthful trends at the beginning because they may be more difficult to talk about later on.

Long-Distance Relationships

Some people arrive at college already in committed relationships. All relationships require communication and nurturance. People who are separated by distance must make sure to give extra attention to communication. This can be difficult for couples that do not have the luxury of seeing each another very often. However, despite not being able to see each other frequently, the challenge of communicating, being honest, and continually getting to know your partner are by no means insurmountable.

Going into the situation aware that an extra commitment to communication is required to make the relationship "work," can actually put some people in a better position than other couples who see each other all the time and take such relational traits for granted. Couples in close proximity have the benefit of having additional opportunities to work on communication – but that does not mean the individuals in the relationship take advantage of such a great luxury. The fortunate thing about long-distance relationships in our contemporary society is that we live in an information age where e-mail, video phones, cell phones, and faxes can help us bridge the distance to the one(s) we love. And let's not forget about the traditional old romantic love letter!

Communication Tip:
Long-distance couples commonly wrestle with issues of trust, attention, and reciprocity—much like all couples! However, it can be more difficult to work through these issues when you are not face-to-face or your time together is limited. Make a conscious effort to set aside regular times to talk to each other. Being verbally honest and open with your feelings is even more important in phone or email conversations because it's not possible to observe body language.

Staying Close Despite Being 600 Miles Apart
Thank goodness for phones and email! My boyfriend and I have been doing the long-distance thing for 1 year and we never knew how good phone sex could be until now! It helps us feel close and be intimate even though we're 600 miles apart. Shaina, 23 years old.

Making a Change in a Long-Distance Relationship
My girlfriend and I go to separate colleges. In the beginning, we were exclusive but it made us both miserable and we both resented each other for "stopping" us from having fun. Eventually we decided that we trusted one another and knew that nothing could damage our friendship if we were honest and open about our experiences. We have both been physical with others at our colleges and we are doing great! Louis, 22 years old.

Breaking Up

There are many ways to break-up. However, there are only certain ways to break-up in accordance with the Sexual Etiquette Guidelines outlined earlier in this book. For example, making threatening phone calls, harming your partner's new relationship, or slashing the tires of his or her car are not healthy, legal, or acceptable ways to treat someone, even if the break-up hurt your feelings. After all, this is a person you supposedly cared about or loved.

Only you will be able to determine the right time to end a relationship. Whether it is a friendship, partnership, or marriage, break-ups often hurt. Of course there are some relationships that end mutually, but even these partners may have to deal with feelings of loss, loneliness, or sadness. Everyone deserves to be treated with respect. If you cannot give that to your partner, or he or she is not providing that for you, it is worth communicating to see if such caring will ever materialize. Life is too short to be with someone who treats you in a neglectful, aggressive, or violent manner. Some couples break-up and get back together numerous times. This is quite normal. Sometimes breaking-up can be too painful to do in one movement. Sometimes couples want to explore what it may feel like to be away from each another for a while. Some couples break-up when they feel smothered or controlled and want to experience the freedom that comes with not being in a relationship. If you feel threatened, intimidated, are harmed during a break-up, or are in an abusive situation, there are resources that may help you (see Chapter 10).

Time To End It

I had what I thought was a great relationship in high school. When we went away to college, we decided to stay together. However, when I got here and started to meet new people, I also started feeling smothered by my old relationship. Telling my boyfriend was one of the hardest things I've ever done, and we both cried a lot; but it was the best thing for both of us. Makayla, 19 years old.

Long-Term Relationships

We each have certain needs, expectations, and hopes for our lives. Sometimes to accomplish our dreams, we must plan early and look ahead to where we would like to be in the future.

Long-term relationships take many of the same skills that are required in dating and friendship. The relationship must be given attention, and the partners involved must communicate continually about their changing needs and desires. Everyone changes over the years, and the best way to assure that you grow with your partner is to check-in with him or her. Think of it as "dating" throughout the span of the relationship.

In order to assess if a partner is best suited for your desires, dreams, and needs, you may want to explore what qualities you would like in a partner. This way, when you select a life partner, husband, lover, or wife, you will be more likely to select someone with qualities, values, beliefs, and behaviors that are closely suited to your individual tastes.

Of course, there are many forms of long-term relationships. While marriage is one of the most common forms, some people live together in an equally committed partnership without the formality of marriage. Others live by themselves, or with friends or family members. Some people are "serially monogamous," meaning they partner with or marry someone for a while and then move on to another relationship after a break-up or divorce.

Whatever your plans for a future relationship(s), the bottom line is that relationships take work. Some people are surprised to hear "after the wedding, the marriage has just begun." A commitment ceremony or wedding is by no means an excuse to stop "dating" or getting to know your partner. People who stay together for a long time in *happy*, mutually satisfying relationships have to work at nurturing one another as well as at the daily tasks of living.

Communication Tip:

There is often a temptation to like and be involved in everything that your partner likes or does. Individuals in relationships need to hold on to their individuality and resist becoming engulfed in the other person or the relationship. You are not helping yourself or the relationship if you surrender the things about yourself that you love. If both partners continue to work on themselves alongside one another as well as working on the partnership, it can help the relationship flourish. In this case, two wholes—not two halves—equals one complete relationship.

Long-Term Relationships

I never thought of my mom and dad as being sexual. But, now, after 35 years of marriage, it makes me smile when I see them holding hands, hugging, or kissing. Their commitment to and love for one another is a power of example in my life. Philip, 26 years old.

Sexual Diversity

People choose to express, or not to express, themselves in different ways. Some people enjoy nibbling, others sucking. Some like to have sex every day while others prefer once a month. Some people enjoy being spanked and some enjoy giving the spanking. As long as you do not violate the rights of others and take care of yourself, whatever you do to express yourself and your sexuality is your right and privilege.

Man, woman, transgendered, gay, straight, lesbian, bisexual, masculine, feminine, androgynous…these are all labels for an identity, like baseball player, musician, or businesswoman. The labels we carry with us, such as what we do for a living or our nationality, partially define us but do not come close to summing up who we are, how we feel, and how we live. We all use labels every day to help us classify and understand the world—who we talk to, who we may be safe around, who we want for friends, and so on. However, when we start to use labels or stereotypes to completely define people, we reduce them to a word which is neither fair nor accurate. Most people do not enjoy being reduced to a word, hobby, job, sexual orientation, or religion. As Walt Whitman wrote *"I contain multitudes."* We all are filled with vast diversity and, hopefully, we are permitted to celebrate all the sides and pieces of our sexual selves!

Sexual diversity captures a theme we have emphasized since the introduction in this book—everyone is a sexual being and expresses their sexuality in different emotional, psychological, and physical ways. In this section, we will talk about several aspects of sexual diversity, including sexual orientation, gender identity, and ability.

Sexual Orientation

Sexual orientation refers to an individual's sexual attraction to and/or love orientation toward members of the other gender, members of the same gender, or members of both genders. Terms commonly used for these different orientations include "straight," "heterosexual," "gay," "lesbian," "homosexual," and "bisexual" or "bi." Contrary to what many of us have been taught, sexual orientation is not as simple as putting people into categories. People contain a variety of attractions and fantasies. Having fantasies about or experiences with members of the same gender, for example, does not necessarily make you gay, lesbian, or bisexual. These words reflect identities which, in turn, reflect an individual's primary sexual and/or love orientation. Some people also may experience their sexual orientation identity as fluid and changing throughout life.

Coming out is a process of acknowledging to yourself and others that you are gay, lesbian, or bisexual. Although heterosexual people go through the process of developing and acting on attractions to members of the other gender, they usually do not have to "come out" as heterosexual. This is because heterosexuality is the assumed "norm" in our society, which often makes it difficult for people to come out as gay, lesbian, bisexual, or questioning.

Fortunately, there are many resources available to provide support for gay, lesbian, bisexual, transgendered (GLBT), or questioning students on college campuses. Most colleges and universities have centers, support groups, and activities that offer a community and safe space for students. Check with your college's website, phone book, or student activities office for more information specific to your school. Also available are:
• National Gay and Lesbian Hotline (1-888-843-4564)
• National Coming Out Project (1-800-866-6263)
• Parents, Families, and Friends of Lesbians and Gays (PFLAG): www.pflag.org
• !Outproud!: www.outproud.com

First Time Meeting
I wasn't "out" to any of my brothers in the frat when I decided to attend one of the meetings of the gay and lesbian group on campus. I had images of permanently being labeled a "fag" if I went. But, to my relief, there were no cameras, no book to sign; instead, the people there were supportive and didn't make any decisions for me about how to approach my homosexuality. Dominic, 21 years old.

A Process of Discovery
I had sex with females in high school and college. Some of the experiences were great and others were bad. In college I had my first gay experience. It was something I was always curious about and, when it happened, I thought it was great. Now I date men almost exclusively. I don't know what this means in terms of a label, but I know what and who I like, and I don't deny my love for men emotionally, physically, or politically. Owen, 25 years old.

I Can Still Hear...
My suitemates were hanging out in the common room, watching television and joking around. I was studying in my room with the door open. I was suddenly distracted by some really negative stereotypes about lesbians. My suitemates did not know that I was gay. It was hard enough for me to understand my homosexuality at that time in my life. I grabbed my books and went to the library. Even though I left the situation, it has taken a long time for me to get past that experience. Kaya, 21 years old.

Coming Out

Coming out is a never-ending process. There are always new people to come out to and new places to come out in. I don't think it gets easier to do. It stops being some deep dark secret and starts becoming this exciting part of your life you want to share with people. April, 24 years old.

Gender Identity

Societies throughout history have recognized and celebrated gender diversity. For example, in some Native American cultures, a "two-spirited" person (a man who takes on traditional female dress, gender roles, and status) is regarded as another gender (neither man nor woman). Two-spirited individuals are often held in high regard and may be considered shamans, people who have great spiritual power. In contrast, most of Western culture continues to recognize two catagories of gender and looks down upon people who vary from the characteristics traditionally associated with "man" and "woman."

The term "transgendered," or "trans" (the more commonly used word), describes a person who reassigns the sex they were labeled at birth or a person whose gender expression is considered by society as nontraditional for their sex. Trans is an umbrella term that encompasses a diverse group of individuals who cross or transcend culturally defined categories of gender. A trans person may or may not choose to pursue body augmentation or transformation through sex reassignment surgery and/or hormone replacement therapy. Some people may choose to cross-dress (dress part- or full-time as another gender than the sex assigned at birth). People cross-dress for many reasons, including comfort, relaxation, and eroticism.

Within the trans community, there are many subidentity groups, or groups of people who have similar characteristics or experiences. A few of the more common ones include female-to-male transsexual or male-to-female transsexual, androgynous, feminine male, masculine female, gender queer, and fem queen.

Is being *trans* the same as being gay?

Not necessarily. The term "trans" refers to a person's internal sense and external expression of their own gender identity, whereas sexual orientation refers to a person's attraction to other people. Nevertheless, the trans community and the gay, lesbian, and bisexual community often intersect because some trans people are also gay lesbian, or bisexual. In addition, they have many issues in common, including coming out to friends and family, lack of access to non-judgmental health care, difficulty maintaining positive self-esteem, and being at risk of harassment or violence.

For more information about the trans community and gender identity:
• International Foundation for Gender Education: www.ifge.org or (781) 894-8340
• Renaissance Transgender Association: www.ren.org
• You may also wish to read *My Gender Workbook*, by Kate Bornstein

An Understanding R.A.

Ever since I was young, I haven't felt like a boy, even though everyone expected me to act and dress like a boy. At school I was picked on, even beat up, and I felt a lot of pressure from my family to "just act normal." When I went away to college, I thought things would be different. When I saw that everything at college was the same as it was at home, I couldn't take it anymore. But one day, my R.A. noticed I was really withdrawn and asked me to stop by to talk. Just being able to talk to one understanding person who was able to listen, offer support, recommend some resources for me, and didn't judge me, helped me get through a very difficult year. Sami, 19 years old.

NOTE: This story is dedicated to Lydia Sausa, who IS that understanding R.A. and has provided support and resources for many college students and people in the trans community. She can be reached via email at lsausa@dolphin.upenn.edu and by phone at (415) 554-0130.

Intersexuality

Intersexuality is a term that describes individuals born with genitals and other physical anatomy that do not correspond with "typical" male or female anatomy. A number of genetic and hormonal conditions can cause the sexual anatomy to develop differently. One estimate by researcher Anne Fausto-Sterling suggests that when all of the contributing medical conditions are taken into account, the total number of people born annually whose bodies differ from standard male or female bodies is about 1 in 100. The Intersex Society of North America is working to create a community for intersexed people and to prevent the many harmful and medically unnecessary surgeries performed on people with atypical sex anatomy. For more information, contact ISNA at www.isna.org

Ability and Sexuality

People who are other-abled (developmentally, psychologically, or physically from injury or illness) often are perceived by our society as nonsexual. Sex is usually associated with youth and physical attractiveness; people who may not "fit the mold" often get ignored. However, while physical disability or illness may alter the way an individual expresses and experiences sexuality, the person is and always will be sexual.

Recently, more information about sexuality is available for people with disabilities. There are a number of websites that offer support, information, and education:

• *www.sexualhealth.com*
• *www.geocities.com/HotSprings/7319/discool.htm*

Sexually and Emotionally Fulfilled

Two years ago, after a car accident that left me paralyzed from the waist down, I thought I'd never have a sex life again. Now, as my boyfriend and I celebrate our one-year anniversary, I've never been more fulfilled both sexually and emotionally. Together, we have discovered what the term "erogenous zone" really means! Ana, 23 years old.

Love

Love is an abstract concept that is defined differently by various people and cultures. However, according to the Sexual Etiquette Guidelines, there are some things that would be difficult—if not impossible—to include in the category of "love." For example, if a person is humiliated, degraded, ignored, and controlled by a partner yet claimed it was "love," those qualities would not be considered "loving" according to the Guidelines. Behaviors such as violence, intimidation, neglect, and other actions that violate an individual's right to happiness and health are not based on love.

Love may include a wide variety of characteristics—caring, support, listening, being there for each other, commitment, giving each other space to grow. What is important to you in a loving relationship may not be the same for someone else. Therefore, it's helpful to identify your needs for and definition of love.

Love is a beautiful and powerful force; however, it does not protect any of us. It is a myth that if we are "in love" that somehow intercourse will be more beautiful, pure, and safe than if we had intercourse with someone we did not love. The fact is, unprotected intercourse is unprotected intercourse. High-risk behavior is high-risk behavior. Sexually transmitted infections do not think to themselves, "well, they are in love so I'll leave them alone." Even people who are in love must take precautions to protect themselves from the possible negative health consequences of sexual behavior.

Jealousy is a blend of different emotions that are frequently associated with love. Many consider jealousy a single emotion when, in fact, it tends to be a mixture of many emotions, such as feeling threatened, hurt, insecure, afraid, and angry. Many people use the word "jealousy" to describe some of these feelings.

Jealousy and love do NOT go hand in hand. Loving someone does not mean that you must feel insecure, threatened, or jealous. There are certain behaviors that are guaranteed to make a partner feel caged, controlled, intimidated, and dissatisfied. Not letting a partner enjoy his or her hobbies, denying him or her the right to relationships and connections with friends and family, and trying to dictate behavior, dress, and feelings are several examples of this type of behavior. Jealousy can cause many complications and feelings of dissatisfaction within a relationship. Since people exhibiting jealous feelings generally want their partners to stay with them, it is ironic that they would treat their partners poorly. Often the best way to handle jealousy is to communicate about the source of those feelings and what you as a couple could do to help one another feel more comfortable and trusting.

I Got Through My Jealousy

I was so jealous that I used to call my girlfriend a slut for just hugging or saying hi to another guy. Eventually, my insecurities threatened my friendship and relationship with her. I did not want to lose her so I decided to do something about it. I went to a counselor on campus and he told me that my behavior would only push her away. He was right—my being a jealous jerk who wouldn't let her do anything would only make her break up with me. After a little while, I relaxed and trusted her and quit controlling her and insulting her. The best way to keep a girlfriend is definitely to treat her with respect, caring, and praise! I am thrilled we are still together and we are closer than ever and she is so happy that she is no longer dating a bully. I am proud of myself. Cordel, 23 years old.

Pleasure

When it comes to sexual pleasure, we live in a culture that frequently sends mixed messages. On the one hand, sexual pleasure is glorified in the media. People are shown in movies having casual sex without consequences, professional athletes go public with the number of sex partners they've had, and sexual images are everywhere in print and on TV. On the other hand, however, most children grow up in families in which sex is viewed as secretive, embarrassing, or even shameful. Furthermore, there are differences in the messages girls and boys receive about pleasure. For example, it is more common for boys to learn that masturbation is normal and expected, while for girls masturbation frequently is not talked about or is condemned as wrong. These messages can affect adult sexual behavior. For example, women may have problems experiencing orgasm or feeling sexual desire. To the contrary, men may experience problems with early or rapid ejaculation related to the way in which they learned about pleasure and masturbation (e.g., do it quickly and don't get caught).

There's no doubt that the emotional, psychological, and relationship components of sexual activity are important, but there is something to be said about getting in touch with pleasure. As human beings, we tend to avoid things that cause pain and pursue things that are pleasurable. Sexual activity can be one of those enjoyable things. Enjoying the positive aspects of sex has the potential to increase self-esteem, help a person get in touch with his or her body, aid in relaxation, and bring closeness and intimacy to a relationship—not to mention, sexual pleasure can be fun!

Although the terms may sound similar, there is a difference between sexual *desire* and sexual *pleasure*.

• *Sexual desire is the emotional and physical yearning for sexual activity.*
• *Sexual pleasure involves the positive emotional and physical feelings experienced during sexual activity.*

In order to embrace the pleasurable part of sexuality, it is important to get informed about the potential negative consequences so that you can make decisions that will lead to positive outcomes. Knowing yourself and your values will also help you stay on a pleasurable path. For example, if you choose to engage in a sexual behavior that is in line with your values, it will probably be more pleasurable than if it conflicts with them, which usually causes guilt or shame.

What About Pleasure?

I have been in a relationship for 3 years with someone I love very much. The relationship started out based purely on sex, which was great in the beginning. But as the relationship became more committed and the stress of school increased, sex decreased and became less pleasurable. We hear a lot about scientific info on sex, but the pleasurable aspect still seems like it's taboo. Isn't learning about increasing pleasure and reducing stress important, too? Sherice, 20 years old

Abstinence...it's more than "just say no"

People abstain from a variety of things for many different reasons. Abstaining from sexual intercourse is a wonderful decision for those who are not ready or do not want to engage in certain sexual behaviors for personal, moral, or religious reasons. If used perfectly, abstinence is the most effective method in preventing sexually transmitted infections or unplanned pregnancy. However, because abstinence involves human beings, there is a chance of this method failing. For example, many people go to parties with every intention of being abstinent. Then, four beers or two joints later, they can't even pronounce abstinence much less practice it consistently and correctly. Abstinence is not magic—it only works as well as the person using it!

What exactly does abstinence mean? This is an important question because different "abstinent" people may not even have the same definition. Lack of a clear definition of what is and is not "allowed" can contribute to confusion and make abstinence less effective in preventing sexually transmitted infections and pregnancy. It may be valuable to explore your friend's, family's, and partner's definitions of abstinence. Is kissing okay? Is mutual masturbation okay? Is grinding okay? Discovering what is acceptable and mutually agreeable to the people involved is always a valuable investment.

If you are interested in being abstinent, the most important thing is to commit yourself to this course of action. You will also need certain skills and tools. Also, you'll need to know when you will be in a possible sexual situation. It's important to have a positive vision for the future, as well as confidence in your values and beliefs, awareness of your options, and good limit-setting and communication skills.

Finally, you will need to have a partner who agrees to abstain to the specific behaviors you have decided constitute abstinence. In the end, know that abstinence—just like using birth control or safer sex— takes work, commitment, and self-respect. If all of these are in place, abstinence will work for you as a choice that can make you proud of yourself.

Communication Tip:

Surveys show that people have a wide variety of opinions of what is abstinence and what is sex. For example, in 1991, of 600 students at a Midwestern university, 59% did not believe that oral sex would qualify as "sex" and only 19% thought anal sex would qualify as "sex." All the more reason to be clear with yourself and your partner about the definitions of abstinence and sex! *Source: Sanders, S.A. & Reinisch, J.M. (1999). Would you say you "had sex" if...? Journal of the American Medical Association, 281 (3), 274-277.*

Not Having Sex Cleared My Mind

For the last 4 months I have chosen to not participate in any sexual behavior and have been completely successful. It definitely cleared my mind and has allowed me to focus my concentration on friendships with females. I find it easier to really get to know a female when there are no expectations of performance. I've found that sex isn't really necessary for a loving relationship. I feel more confident because of my decision. Thuy, 22 years old.

Deciding Not to Have Intercourse

My boyfriend and I were together for about 3 months when we started having sex. We are both very paranoid and we always use a condom with spermicide. That wasn't good enough for me so I began looking at other methods, such as the pill and Depo Provera, to use with the condoms. He decided he would rather not have sex than see me take responsibility for pills or shots. So, we decided not to have intercourse any more. It was not out of religious reasons. Both of us believe that sex-before-marriage is absolutely acceptable. We just decided that we would be less stressed out about pregnancy if we didn't have intercourse. We have abstained for over three months and we are both happy about our decision. We realized that pregnancy is not something that needs to be on our minds with all that is going on at school. I was surprised at my boyfriend's suggestion to stop having intercourse. Neither of us are prudes. We just realized we could make one another happy in many ways without having intercourse. Kirsi, 18 years old.

Outercourse

Many people have heard of intercourse, but few have heard of outercourse. In our culture "sex" is often portrayed as being all or none—either intercourse or abstinence. But the fact is, there is an incredibly diverse middle area between intercourse and abstinence that needs to be given more attention and validation. There are many hot and sexy things people can do with and to one another that do not put anyone at risk for unintended pregnancy, HIV, or other problems that sometimes result from oral, anal, or vaginal intercourse. Such things can be called "outercourse."

Some people call outercourse "foreplay." The word "foreplay" implies that the behaviors come before the "real action" and cannot stand alone as ends in and of themselves. Some people view foreplay as a chore, and only do it to get to "the good stuff." However, outercourse is not something that you have to do only on the way to intercourse. Outercourse is something people do because it feels good and can be fun to share with a partner. For instance, imagine a fantastic and passionate kiss with someone. That kiss does not have to lead to intercourse to be meaningful. To some people, kissing could be incredibly intimate, personal, and pleasurable while to another person intercourse could be meaningless. Intimacy, pleasure, and behaviors do not always correspond with one another. There are a lot of safe options that do not involve intercourse — oral, anal, or vaginal — that you and your partner can do if you want to pleasure one another.

How could anyone do things like kissing, massaging, showering together, telling each other their fantasies, or mutual masturbation and not end up having intercourse? People can control themselves and will do so if they are committed to their limits. However, if you know you won't be able to stop yourself at a certain point, or you don't think your partner will stop him or herself, don't do the behavior that you find uncontrollable. Some people could shower together naked and not have intercourse while other people cannot stop themselves when they kiss. You must know yourself and your partner, as well as learn to communicate your limits.

Lastly, we must start to consider outercourse one of the major methods of contraception. Outercourse can help people enjoy one another without being at risk for some of the negative outcomes of intercourse. It is a method that, if used consistently and in a manner that avoids exchange of semen, vaginal fluids, or contact with infected areas of skin, is also 100% effective against unplanned pregnancy and sexually transmitted infection. It can be brought with us everywhere we go, and is free—just like abstinence!

Intercourse

In this book, when the phrase "sexual intercourse" is used, it includes oral, vaginal, and anal intercourse. These behaviors involve placing the penis inside of the vagina or anus, or, in the case of oral intercourse, putting the penis in the mouth or the mouth on the vulva. In addition, these behaviors have been classified as "intercourse" because they involve possible exchange of body fluids. People of all sexual orientations can engage in various types of sexual intercourse and every person has certain preferences or dislikes for specific behaviors.

Oral intercourse on a male is called *fellatio*—also known, among other terms, as "blow job," "giving head," or "going down." Oral intercourse on a female is called *cunnilingus*—also known, among other terms, as "eating out," or "going down." *Vaginal intercourse* involves inserting a penis into a vagina. Some people may also use a dildo, finger(s), or vibrator. *Anal intercourse* involves inserting the penis into the anus. Some people may also use a dildo, finger(s), or butt plug. It is important not to insert anything into the anus unless it has a flared base (so that it will not get stuck inside the rectum). It is also important to use a water-based lubricant during anal intercourse. The anus, unlike the vagina or mouth, is not self-lubricating. Using water-based lubricants is also recommended during vaginal intercourse when using latex condoms for additional lubrication and added pleasure. See page 76 for an extensive list of water-based lubricants.

Health Tip: Avoid placing the penis into the vagina after anal intercourse. This can transmit bacteria from the anus to the vagina and cause infection. Never insert anything into the body (vagina, anus, mouth, or anywhere) that is made of glass or that cannot be retrieved.

Intercourse has many possible meanings and outcomes. Some people have intercourse to share something physical with a partner. Some people want to enjoy a friend's company. Some people prefer outercourse to intercourse. Others have negative experiences with intercourse. Only you will be able to decide when and what type of intercourse is right for you and under which circumstances.

If you decide that you are going to have intercourse, you also need to decide to use protection. Remember—if your partner does not ask about protection, chances are that he or she hasn't asked other partners either.

Figuring Out Our Limits

My girlfriend and I have been dating for over 5 months and have both been in some previous bad relationships. We've come to realize that open and honest communication is the foundation of a good relationship. Being able to communicate well has helped us decide that mutual masturbation is as far as we want to go sexually right now. Anita, 20 years old.

My First Kiss

I haven't had my first kiss yet. I never used to think about it, but now I feel that there is a void in my life. Always hearing about people's relationships depresses me. Sometimes I feel something is wrong with me, but I still hope I have enough patience to be sensible. For me, even that first kiss is a big deal. Thom, 18 years old.

Can Fun Put Off Intercourse?

One night my girlfriend presented me with a collar and introduced me to light S&M and bondage. Both of us agree that since we have started playing and doing scenes with each other our sex life has been much richer and entertaining whether the evening ends in intercourse or not. Personally, I'd have stuck with abstinence longer if I'd known about S&M as an outlet for sexual tension. A good scene can give as much pleasure as a long night of sex! Benjamin, 24 years old.

CHAPTER 4:
Obstacles to Positive Sexual Expression

Difficulty Expressing Emotion

The best thing about feelings is that they solely belong to us. We are all born with the capacity to feel great joy, pain, and everything in between. The messages we receive about emotions while growing up will determine how we express our inner-most emotions later in life. The ability to express how we feel will powerfully impact our relationships with others and how we experience sexuality.

Males and females have more in common than many people care to admit. Our media and culture tend to highlight gender differences when, in fact, the similarities are glaring. All people want to be respected, loved, and appreciated and to feel attractive, desired, and valued. Of course, we all have different interests, hobbies, and communication styles; but, overall, we all want universal respect and love.

When we do not receive attention and love to meet our basic needs, we tend to communicate our needs or express ourselves in ways that may demand that people pay attention such as violence, crazy driving, wild hairstyles, or outrageous dress. Without the ability to verbally communicate about our emotions, the powerful feelings inside us will find a way out. If they don't, such things as regret, guilt, shame, anger, loss, pain, and frustration will be turned inward. This is why it is so incredibly important that all people are taught how to communicate their emotions in genuine and meaningful ways.

Alcohol and Other Drugs

For many people, college is the first time away from the watchful eye of parents or other authority figures. Thus, college students are exposed to a wide variety of "first time" experiences, including those involving alcohol and other drugs.

We all are given confusing messages about alcohol and other drugs. Certain drugs are legal and can be bought easily. Some drugs are legal and can only be purchased if you are a certain age. Other drugs are illegal. We are often given reasons why certain drugs are better or worse but may have a difficult time understanding the reasons why some drugs are "great" or at least "acceptable" for us and why some drugs are "bad" for us. In the end, it is not necessarily the drug(s) that someone does as much as that person's relationship to the drug(s).

There is no doubt that drug addiction and chemical dependency dramatically interfere with the ability to express ourselves sexually. College students (and others) often say they use alcohol or other drugs to loosen up, decrease inhibitions, and flirt more openly. Indeed, alcohol is frequently a mainstay at college social events; thus, it's easy for alcohol and sex to get mixed up together. It's in this "mix" that many problems - misunderstanding, regret, lack of protection, and date rape - can occur. If you are planning to drink at a party, tell a friend to stick with you and make sure you make it home safely. Never accept a drink from someone if you haven't seen where it came from, and don't leave your drink unattended. Finally, do not assume consent to sexual activity has been given when alcohol or other drugs are involved.

For information on alcohol and drug abuse, refer to Chapter 10 for Narcotics Anonymous and Alcoholics Anonymous as well as other resources.

Dreams, Goals, and Unexpected Pregnancy

This year was my first and last year at college. One night I went out and partied and got drunk. It was my first time drinking. I ended up with some guy that I did not know. I did not remember much of the night, but a month later I learned that I was pregnant. Yes, the first night I ever drank was also my first intercourse as well. Fortunately, I did not have any infections. All of my life, my mother has expected me to be successful. I was so scared to tell her. It was the most difficult thing I have ever had to do in my life. She told me that she would support whatever decision I made. Even though I was the first person in my family to get into college, I could not get the abortion. I am going to drop out in a month and raise my child. It seems like all of my work in high school was a total waste. Claire, 19 years old.

A Little Help From a Friend

At a party this year, a girl was plastered and I started talking to her. After a while, we found ourselves alone. Assuming that it was time to have sex, she began to come on to me. Instead of going along, I realized she didn't know what she was doing. Instead, we talked about our past relationships and what went wrong with them. Imad, 21 years old.

Taking Risks

It hit me one morning as I was staring into the toilet. Alcohol has played a major role in most of my sexual experiences. I thought it helped me open up and be less inhibited but in the end I realized that drinking has screwed up many of my sexual decisions. I've taken risks while drunk that I never should've taken. Molly, 20 years old.

Violence

We are bombarded with an infinite display of violence in movies, television, and other media. Our culture has a reputation in the world as being more concerned that a child see a bare breast than see someone shot in the head and murdered on a movie screen. Most of us have become so numb and desensitized to violence that, as a culture, we have difficulty recognizing how much extreme violence is present in the shows we watch, the music we listen to, who our heroes are, and the way that people treat one another. This contributes to a false sense of danger. It makes us afraid to let our children play in the street or to help a stranger. It drives us to lock our doors and buy guns, worrying that at any moment we, too, may be a victim of violence. Of course, there are some very real threats in the world and we all must be cautious and vigilant. Nonetheless, the frequency and graphic nature of serial killer movies and television shows all contribute to a collective image of our society as full of violence. These numerous violent images offer unhealthy and illegal ways to solve problems. Some people have only witnessed violence as the way to settle disputes, disagreements, jealousy, and differences instead of healthy dialogue. Honesty and open communication don't sell movie tickets like violence does, but good communication is the foundation of healthy relationships.

Violence does not have to be only physical. Intimidation, threatening, belittling, neglecting, ignoring, and screaming all can be forms of verbal, psychological, and spiritual violence. Physical and emotional violence are not the ways to solve problem—they create more problems. If you are, or have been, a victim of violence in a relationship and want to seek help, contact one of the following hotlines:

Resources:
• Domestic Violence Hotline: 1-800-942-6909
• National Child Abuse Hotline: 1-800-422-4453

I'm a Guy and I Hate Violence...

I am a wrestler and I hate violence. I enjoy athletics but despise fighting and violent acts. My friends would all think I'm weak if I admit that I hate violence. It almost seems like, to be a man, I can't speak out against violence. I don't think I'll be allowed "in the club" if they find out it upsets me. In my heart I believe other guys feel the same way I do but are afraid to admit it for fear of being seen as weak or feminine. Jamal, 22 years old.

He Hit Me...

Half of my junior year and all of my senior year of high school I dated this guy. After we dated for about 2 months we were arguing and he hit me. It got worse as time went on and he made me do a lot of things I didn't want by threatening and intimidating me. I didn't tell anyone and I didn't deal with it well. After I finally got the courage to leave, it took me a long time to commit again. But, now I know what I would do if anyone ever mistreated me in a relationship and I will teach my future children what to do as well. Christi, 21 years old.

Hazing

Because hazing is prevalent on college campuses, we have included it in the category of violence. The reason for this is that it can be an aggressive act that constitutes verbal, physical, or psychological violence and intimidation. Sometimes hazing can involve unwanted or unintended sexual behaviors.

The military is based on a model that often humiliates and degrades people. Sometimes people convince themselves that such a style of learning is appropriate outside the military. In the military, people are preparing for war and need to strengthen their ability to kill other people and bear up under hardship. Clearly, every day society is not war or the military. Degrading and screaming at people is no way to build camaraderie.

Traditions can occur around anything. Some time ago a tradition of violent and dangerous hazing began to be perpetuated on college campuses. This has included such activities as forced excessive drinking, taking unnecessary or dangerous risks, physical harm, or harming others. Acts of violent hazing do not follow the Sexual Etiquette Guidelines and are not healthy. Nothing could be more disturbing than having your son, daughter, or friend die because of a prank or so-called rite of initiation; yet, it continues to happen. Many colleges are starting to recognize the destructive nature of such behavior and have begun to outline consequences for irresponsible actions involving the mistreatment of human beings. Colleges are doing their part to make sure that all students and organizations abide by some basic universal principals of treatment.

A Single Night...

I am a freshman and, before I came here, I thought I would never have sex before marriage, but that all changed one night at a fraternity party. I was drinking a lot and guys were buying me drinks. I even did a beer funnel to the cheers of many of the guys there. I was having a good time all night when all of a sudden the night seemed to end. I had no idea what happened or what I had done that night. That's what scared me. My whole life I believed one thing and in just one night it all changed. Melissa, 20 years old.

Negative Messages About Sexuality

Everyone has different values, beliefs, and attitudes about sexuality. As we grow up, we are given many messages. Some people get messages that their sexual body parts are dirty, or that pleasure is bad, and nudity is shameful. These messages continue to build up until they have suppressed our ability to feel proud of our desires, fantasies, and ourselves as sexual beings. All of this contributes to feelings of guilt and shame. Unfortunately, women seem to suffer more than men, due to messages that they must be "pure", meaning asexual. It takes many women decades to shed only a fragment of the controlling messages telling them to be modest, innocent, and "appropriate."

It is difficult to break free of these messages—some subtly, some overt—that build up and pollute our overall sense of health and comfort. Sometimes the negative messages about sexuality are so extreme that all pleasure or joy is seen as disgusting. Some individuals may need to seek professional help to "unlearn" the negative conditioning they learned about sexuality.

People who believe that fantasies are "wrong" and sexual pleasure is not an acceptable motivation for being with a partner tend to have greater sexual dissatisfaction. Feelings of shame and fear of pleasure can contribute to difficulties experiencing orgasm and other problems. If you are struggling with negative messages about sexuality, it may be helpful to discuss your feelings with a sex or relationship therapist. To find a therapist in your area, contact the American Association of Sex Educators, Counselors, and Therapists (AASECT) at www.aasect.org. Many colleges and universities also have specially trained counselors to help students deal with sexuality and relationship issues. Ask at your student health center for more information.

Silence Breeds Trouble

I was brought up in a very conservative household in which nothing was ever talked about. Since the first time I had intercourse, I have yet to have an experience while not under the influence of some type of drug and two of these "experiences" were unwanted. I have never felt comfortable enough to talk to anyone about sex and I usually end up feeling sad and alone after a sexual experience. I hope that someday I will be able to move past the shame and low self-esteem associated with my sexuality. Cam, 18 years old.

CHAPTER 5:
Contraception and Safer Sex

Why Contraception and Safer Sex?

Did you know that 50% of all pregnancies in the United States are unintended? Also, did you know that 1 in 4 individuals will contract a sexually transmitted infection (STI) in their lifetime? These statistics are a sobering reminder of the potential consequences of sexual behavior. Fortunately, there are things you can do to help prevent these negative outcomes from affecting your life and relationships. In this chapter, we will discuss methods of contraception and safer sex. We hope you will use this information to help make the decisions that are best for you.

Every woman who engages in vaginal intercourse is at risk of becoming pregnant. Likewise, every individual who engages in oral, anal, or vaginal intercourse (and sometimes other behaviors that bring infected skin into contact with infected skin) is at potential risk of getting an STI. A contraceptive is any technique, method, or device that reduces the risk of a woman becoming pregnant. There are also some methods, including contraceptives, which reduce the likelihood of transmitting infection. These are called methods of safer sex. The word "safer" is used instead of "safe" because even though some approaches are highly effective, there is still a chance that the method might fail. Remember that the only guaranteed way to avoid pregnancy and infection is to not engage at all in the behaviors that put you at risk.

Choosing a contraceptive method can be a complicated decision. Each has a varying degree of effectiveness, advantages, and disadvantages. In addition, some contraceptives offer non-contraceptive benefits along with reducing the risk of pregnancy and infection. Reduced rates of certain types of cancer as well as reduced menstrual bleeding, cramping, and premenstrual syndrome (PMS) in women are just a few of the non-contraceptive benefits of modern contraception.

Every sexually active individual can benefit from the consistent and correct use of contraception. Unfortunately, though contraceptives provide many advantages, they are not always easy to use. They can be complicated or messy. They require planning and open communication. They may not be with you every time you need them, and even when everything is done exactly as it should be done, no contraceptive (including abstinence) is 100% effective. Even abstinence may **not** be 100% effective because individuals trying to be abstinent could change their minds, have differing definitions of what is considered abstinence, use alcohol or other drugs, or be pressured or forced into sexual activity.

Knowing both the advantages and disadvantages of all available contraceptive methods can help you make an educated decision about the best method for you. Taking measures to protect you and your partner against unintended pregnancy and STIs offers peace of mind that can help make sex more enjoyable as well as protect your health and well-being.

Choosing the Right Contraception

If you have decided to use contraception, you have taken an important step towards sexual responsibility. With so many choices, trying to choose the right method can be intimidating. Here are a few points to keep in mind when making contraceptive decisions:

• *Usually, you will be able to use the methods YOU want*
• *Each contraceptive method has both advantages and disadvantages*
• *Effectiveness and safety are important concerns*
• *Protection against STIs and HIV needs to be considered*
• *Convenience and ability to use the method correctly are important*
• *The most effective method is usually the one you use consistently and correctly*
• *Negotiation with your partner may be important*
• *Take into consideration how the method will affect the menstrual cycle*
• *Other factors (religion, privacy, past experience) may affect your choice*
• *The best method is ultimately the one YOU choose and use*

Respect My Need for Protection

I have always used protection—a condom—with all of my previous partners even though I am on the pill. My current boyfriend and I decided that since we were both tested and, since I have a bad reaction to the spermicide on condoms, that we would just rely on my birth control pills. Three months later he casually told me about a girl he and his friends had sex with at spring break. He had not used condoms. We have both been tested twice since and the results were negative. Still, my lifetime of perfect contraception use and protection against infection could have been destroyed in those few acts by my boyfriend. He only forgot one sexual experience and could have killed me in the process. I wonder what would happen if he ever lied to me. Now I think that unprotected sex is not worth it even though it feels better. I would never do it again, nor would I date anyone who did not respect my need for protection. Marilee, 26 years old.

4-Wheel Drive Boyfriend to the Rescue

Last winter I had just started seeing a guy, who is now my boyfriend. I had gotten sick and on top of that, it was snowing. I was out of pills. I called him because he had a car with 4-wheel drive and even though I was embarrassed, asked him if he would go to the drug- store for me to pick up my pills. He went, and from then on, discussions about contracep- tives were easy. He later admitted that he was pretty embarrassed, but so was I, so I guess we were equal. We had had sex before then, but never really talked about anything. We talk about everything now! Sex has gotten better and better after learning to be open. Rathi, 20 years old.

A Little Too Late...

When deciding on whether to have sex or not, the main problem was that my girlfriend didn't want to get pregnant. She also did not want to have to go through her mother to get birth control. So, we decided to have unprotected sex and she got pregnant. She decided to have an abortion. Then, she went to her mother and asked for birth control. Dwight, 18 years old.

Making Contraception and Safer Sex Work For You

Data on contraceptive effectiveness are presented in two ways: perfect-use and typical-use failure rates. *Perfect-use failure rate* means the percentage of people who start using a method and use it perfectly (both consistently and correctly) who experience an accidental pregnancy during the first year. *Typical-use failure rate* means the percentage of people who start using a method and who use it perfectly as well as incorrectly and inconsistently (e.g., forgetting to take a pill, not using condoms every time) who experience an accidental pregnancy during the first year. Typical users are more likely to experience contraceptive failure than perfect users.

Whichever method of contraception you ultimately choose, you must feel comfortable enough with your decision and the method itself to use it perfectly every time. Consistent, correct, and careful use of contraception often requires cooperation between both partners. Comfort and confidence in contraceptive methods are essential for successful use. Finally, remember that many of the methods are reversible, which means you can change your mind. You may try different methods before you find the one that is right for you.

How do you feel about your specific contraceptive options? Use the questions below to help you compare the various methods.

Contraceptive Comfort and Confidence Scale:

Very	Somewhat	Not at all	Don't know
1	2	3	?

_____ *Do I object to this method?*
_____ *Does my partner object to this method?*
_____ *Does my religion object to this method?*
_____ *Will I or my partner be embarrassed by using this method?*
_____ *Will it bother me if this method interrupts sexual activity?*
_____ *Will I enjoy sexual activity less because of this method?*
_____ *Does this method cost too much?*
_____ *Will this method cause health problems for me or my partner?*
_____ *Have I or my partner had problems and/or a pregnancy using this method?*
_____ *Will this method negatively affect the menstrual cycle?*
_____ *Will I have trouble remembering to use this method?*
_____ *Will I have trouble using this method carefully?*
_____ *Will I have trouble using this method correctly?*
_____ *Will I have trouble using this method consistently each and every time I have sex?*

"Don't know" answers suggest a need for more thought, introspection, or communication between you and your partner, or more information. A low score (14-21) may mean that you might not like or be successful with the method, whereas high scores (36-42) suggest that the method may be right for you. Scores in the middle range (22-35) suggest that you need to carefully consider whether the method will be suitable since using it will require concerted effort.

The contraceptives presented in this chapter are arranged in alphabetical order as follows:

CONTRACEPTIVE OPTIONS:

Abstinence

The first step in considering the subject of abstinence is defining it! The definitions are fairly clear in terms of preventing pregnancy and infection. In terms of contraception, abstinence from the activity that causes pregnancy is abstinence from vaginal-penile intercourse. When it comes to protecting yourself from infection, abstinence means not engaging in vaginal, anal, and oral intercourse, and any other activity (such as grinding) that might bring body fluids or infected areas of skin into contact. In terms of infections such as herpes, this may also mean abstaining from activities like kissing (if you have herpes lesions - cold sores - on your lips).

How effective is abstinence in preventing pregnancy?
Perfect use failure rate: **0%**
Typical use failure rate: Exact percentage unknown; dependent on individual/couple

How much does abstinence cost?: Free

What are the advantages of abstinence?
• Always available. Abstinence requires no special materials or devices to work perfectly, only two willing partners.
• Highly effective in preventing pregnancy when used perfectly (that is, 100% of the time, no exceptions). Abstinence is the single most effective method of birth control.
• Reduces risk of STIs (depending on the other sexual activities involved).
• Inexpensive.
• Can be started any time.
• Can increase self-esteem. Those who choose to abstain may feel a justifiable sense of pride in their decision. In addition, many religions and cultures endorse abstinence at some point during people's lives.
• Can strengthen relationships. A mutual decision to abstain from sexual intercourse can increase the emotional closeness of two partners.

What are the disadvantages of abstinence?
• Partners may not be prepared to use contraception and safer sex methods if they decide later on to have sexual intercourse.
• Some people find not having intercourse too frustrating and may feel as though they are "missing out."
• A decision by only one partner to abstain may cause conflict between the partners.
• May be difficult to use consistently. Maintaining your decision to abstain can be very challenging in certain high-pressure or passionate situations.
• If only abstaining from penis-in-vagina intercourse, there may be no protection against infections transmitted through other activities such as oral or anal intercourse, including herpes, genital warts, and HIV/AIDS.

How do I choose to be and remain abstinent?

1. Discuss your decision to abstain openly with your partner in the beginning of the relationship and periodically thereafter.
2. Discuss in advance—when you feel clearheaded, sober, and good about yourself—which activities you will abstain from and why.
3. Identify alternative activities to express intimacy. Abstinence does not mean refraining from all sexual activity. People who abstain from intercourse (as well as those who engage in intercourse) may find holding hands, dancing, massaging, kissing, solo masturbation, mutual masturbation, and fantasy as erotic as sexual intercourse. Know that you can remain abstinent and be erotic and sexual. Creativity is the key!
4. Identify possible roadblocks to abstinence and strategies to overcome them.
5. Work together to set sexual limits and communicate them during sexual activity. Learn to say "no" and mean it. It is your right and responsibility to say "no," to say it emphatically, and to repeat it if necessary. You do not have to give a reason for your decision, although you may choose to do so. If you feel threatened or unsafe in any way, leave the scene, or better yet, avoid such situations. Abstinence is your decision, and you do not have to justify it to anyone.
6. Continue to discuss your commitment to abstinence with your partner throughout your relationship.
7. Get information about safer sex and have methods of contraception and STI protection on hand in case the time comes when you decide not to abstain.
8. Know that emergency contraception is available if you were not able to or decided not to abstain and did not use protection.
9. Be proud of your commitment—whether it's based on values or a desire to prevent unintended pregnancy or infection, you're doing something healthy and right for you!

Cervical Cap

The cervical cap is a thimble-shaped latex rubber device. The woman puts spermicide (which kills sperm) in the cap and then places it into her vagina and onto her cervix (the opening of the uterus). The cap forms a seal over the cervix so sperm cannot enter the uterus. Caps come in four sizes.

How effective is the cervical cap?

Perfect use failure rate: **9%** in a woman who has never had a child
                                  26% in a woman who has had a child
Typical use failure rate: **20%** in a woman who has not had a child
                                  40% in a woman who has had a child

[Source: Trussell, J., Contraceptive Technology, 1998]

How much does the cervical cap cost?
Between $20-$30 for the cap, plus an office/clinic visit and spermicide (one cap lasts for 3 years)

What are the advantages of the cervical cap?
• The cervical cap is small and easy to carry.
• It can be placed in the vagina up to 6 hours before intercourse and should remain at least 6 hours after the last ejaculation and no longer than 48 hours.
• It can remain in place for multiple acts of intercourse for up to 48 hours.
• It does not matter how many times you have sex as long as you leave it in at least 6 hours after the last time you have sex.
• Your partner doesn't have to know you are using it.
• In the process of learning how to use the cervical cap, a woman learns a lot about her own anatomy.
• It holds back menstrual blood during intercourse. Hoever, using the cervical cap during menstruation is not generally recommended because of the risk of toxic shock syndrome.

What are the disadvantages of the cervical cap?
• No protection against STIs, including HIV.
• You must be fitted for a cervical cap by a clinician.
• You should wash your hands with soap and water before putting your cap in.
• Inserting the cap may interrupt sex.
• Using the cap increases your risk for inflammation of the surface of the cervix.
• Some women do not like placing fingers or a foreign body into the vagina.
• It is difficult for some women to insert a cervical cap properly.
• If left in too long, the cap increases slightly your risk for a very serious infection called toxic shock syndrome. Don't leave your cervical cap in for more than 48 hours.
• The cap might not be placed onto the cervix properly or it may slip out of place during sex.
• A new fitting may be necessary after having a baby, an abortion, miscarriage, or gaining 15 pounds.
• Latex (rubber) may cause irritation or a woman may be allergic to it.
• Odor may develop if the cervical cap is left in place too long, if not appropriately cleansed, or if used during bacterial vaginosis infection.
• Relatively high failure rate.
• Severe obesity may make it difficult for the patient to place cap correctly.

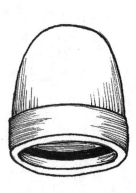
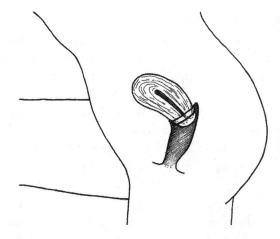

How do I use the cervical cap?

1. See your clinician to get fitted for a cap.
2. *To put the cervical cap in,* fill the bottom third of the cap with spermicide and insert the cap before intercourse. The dome of the cap should completely cover the cervix. The rim of the cap should be tucked snugly and evenly into the areas where the cervix meets the vaginal wall. Make a sweep with your finger around the entire cervix to make sure there is a tight fit. After it fits in place for about one minute, the cap should not dislodge with pressure.
3. Insert the cap up to 6 hours before intercourse.
4. Keep the cap in for 6 hours after intercourse.
5. *To remove the cervical cap,* insert a finger into the vagina until you feel the rim of the cap. Press the cap rim until the seal against the cervix is broken; then tilt the cap off the cervix. Hook finger around the rim and pull the cap sideways out of the vagina. Wash, rinse, and dry the cap and store it in a cool, dark, and dry location.
6. Rinsing the cap in mouth wash can help prevent odor build up.
7. If you have sex more than once, there is no need to add more spermicide, but you should check to make sure the cap is still in place before having sex again.
8. Do not leave the cap in for more than 48 hours if you have an infection or during your period because it increases your risk of toxic shock syndrome.
9. Do not expose the cap to oil-based products such as vaseline, baby oil, yeast infection creams, and oil-based antibiotic creams.
10. Use a back-up method the first few times until you are confident in your use of the cap.
11. Combining the cap and the male or female condom can increase protection against pregnancy and infection.
12. Alcohol and other drug use can reduce the effectiveness of the cervical cap. Being drunk or using other drugs increases the risk of making a mistake.
13. The FDA recommends a follow-up Pap smear after 3 months of use.
14. Do not use the cap for at least 2 or 3 days before routine gynecological exams because it can interfere with the Pap smear. Use a different method if needed.
15. If the cap dislodges, emergency contraception is available. Call 1-888-NOT-2-LATE.

Condoms for Men

Condoms are made of latex (often called "rubbers"), polyurethane (plastic), or natural membranes (often called "lambskins" and made from the sheep intestines). Polyurethane condoms may be used by couples when either partner is allergic to latex. Latex condoms are the most common type available. Condoms look like long thin balloons before they are blown up. Condoms act as a physical barrier; they stop sperm from going into the vagina and prevent numerous infections by inhibiting the exchange of body fluids. The condom must be put onto the penis before the penis comes into contact with the vagina.

How effective are male latex condoms at preventing pregnancy?

Perfect use failure rate: **3%**

Typical use failure rate: **14%**   [Trussel, J., Contraceptive Technology, 1998]

NOTE: Whether condoms lubricated with spermicides are more effective than other lubricated condoms in protecting against the transmission of HIV and other STDs has not been determined.

How much do male condoms cost?

Cost ranges from free at many clinics to several dollars for a designer condom. Average retail cost of a latex condom is 50 cents and for the polyurethane Avanti condom is $2.00. A box of natural skin condoms costs about $20.00.

What are the advantages of male condoms?

• Condoms are safe and effective at preventing both pregnancy and infection when they are used during each act of sex.
• Sexual intercourse may be enjoyed more because there is less fear of STIs, HIV, and pregnancy.
• Guys "last longer" when they use condoms. Prolonging sex may make sex more fun.
• Condoms come in many colors, flavors, sizes, and with or without ribbing. Variety can be exciting!
• Condoms make intercourse less messy by collecting the ejaculate.
• If a guy's partner puts the condom on for him, it can be fun for both partners!
• If you use a water-based lubricant such as Astroglide or KY Jelly, you may decrease the chance that your condom will break.
• To decrease the chance of the condom sliding down the penis or slipping into the vagina or anus, hold the rim of the condom and pull the penis out of the vagina or anus right after ejaculation. Don't continue thrusting until the penis becomes soft.

- Practice putting a condom onto a banana or your penis. This will make it easier to use condoms during sex.
- With condoms, the risk of infertility for female partners is decreased.
- Condoms may reduce the risk of cervical cancer because there's less risk of HPV infection.
- A visit to a clinic or doctor's office is not required to start using condoms.
- Condoms are fairly easy to get and usually do not cost a lot.
- Condoms are a good contraceptive option to use with other methods as a backup or for STI protection.
- Condoms are immediately reversible; once you stop using condoms, pregnancy is possible.

What are the disadvantages of male condoms?
- Unless one partner puts a condom on as a part of outercourse, the condom may interrupt sex.
- Condoms require some practice to learn how to use.
- When putting the condom on the penis you must avoid tearing the condom or putting a hole in it with fingernails, a ring or anything sharp. This includes any thing sharp in the mouth such as braces or piercings!
- YOU CAN'T USE OIL BASED LUBRICANTS such as Vaseline, sun tan oil, whipped cream, or Crisco with latex condoms! These products can put a hole in a latex condom in a matter of seconds.
- Some guys cannot maintain an erection with a condom on.
- The guy must pull out soon after ejaculation. If he becomes soft, the condom can fall off and be left in the vagina or anus without the couple knowing this has happened.
- Some people are sensitive (or allergic) to latex or find the smell very unpleasant.
- Buying, negotiating use, putting on, and getting rid of condoms may be embarrassing for some people. (NOTE: You probably don't want your first time using a condom to be the first time you want to use it with a partner. It is recommended that you practice on yourself, your fingers, or another object beforehand.)
- Condoms can decrease enjoyment of sex by causing decreased sensation for either partner.
- Condoms may not be available when you need one.

Warning: Condoms Clog Toilets!
Once during high school I had sex with this girl I was dating. It was the first time I used a condom. We were at her house so afterwards we were worried about where to throw the condom away. Her parents were coming home soon and we didn't want to leave it in her room. I decided to flush it down the toilet, but when I did it clogged the toilet somehow. We had to get dressed quickly and run down the stairs to tell her dad that I had clogged the toilet. Her parents paid a plumber $200 to find out their daughter was having intercourse! I was pretty embarrassed but she and I still laugh about it. Mark, 20 years old.

How do I use male condoms?

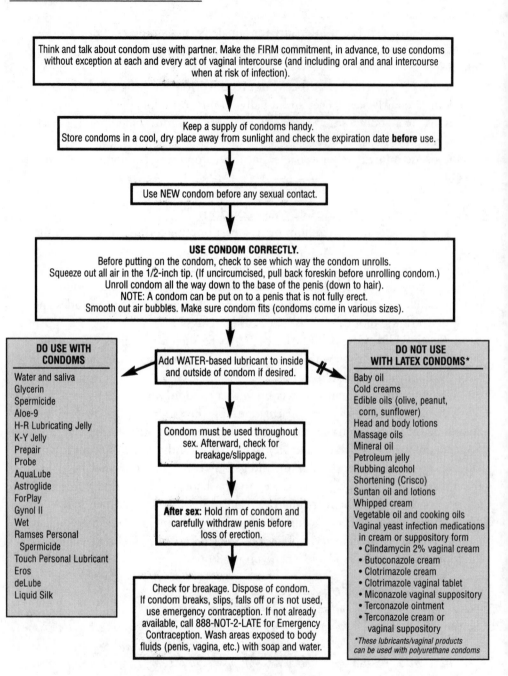

Think and talk about condom use with partner. Make the FIRM commitment, in advance, to use condoms without exception at each and every act of vaginal intercourse (and including oral and anal intercourse when at risk of infection).

Keep a supply of condoms handy.
Store condoms in a cool, dry place away from sunlight and check the expiration date **before** use.

Use NEW condom before any sexual contact.

USE CONDOM CORRECTLY.
Before putting on the condom, check to see which way the condom unrolls.
Squeeze out all air in the 1/2-inch tip. (If uncircumcised, pull back foreskin before unrolling condom.)
Unroll condom all the way down to the base of the penis (down to hair).
NOTE: A condom can be put on to a penis that is not fully erect.
Smooth out air bubbles. Make sure condom fits (condoms come in various sizes).

DO USE WITH CONDOMS

Water and saliva
Glycerin
Spermicide
Aloe-9
H-R Lubricating Jelly
K-Y Jelly
Prepair
Probe
AquaLube
Astroglide
ForPlay
Gynol II
Wet
Ramses Personal Spermicide
Touch Personal Lubricant
Eros
deLube
Liquid Silk

Add WATER-based lubricant to inside and outside of condom if desired.

Condom must be used throughout sex. Afterward, check for breakage/slippage.

After sex: Hold rim of condom and carefully withdraw penis before loss of erection.

Check for breakage. Dispose of condom. If condom breaks, slips, falls off or is not used, use emergency contraception. If not already available, call 888-NOT-2-LATE for Emergency Contraception. Wash areas exposed to body fluids (penis, vagina, etc.) with soap and water.

DO NOT USE WITH LATEX CONDOMS*

Baby oil
Cold creams
Edible oils (olive, peanut, corn, sunflower)
Head and body lotions
Massage oils
Mineral oil
Petroleum jelly
Rubbing alcohol
Shortening (Crisco)
Suntan oil and lotions
Whipped cream
Vegetable oil and cooking oils
Vaginal yeast infection medications in cream or suppository form
• Clindamycin 2% vaginal cream
• Butoconazole cream
• Clotrimazole cream
• Clotrimazole vaginal tablet
• Miconazole vaginal suppository
• Terconazole ointment
• Terconazole cream or vaginal suppository
These lubricants/vaginal products can be used with polyurethane condoms

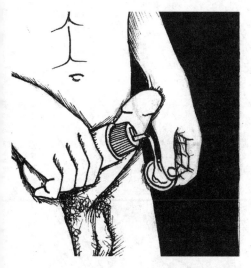

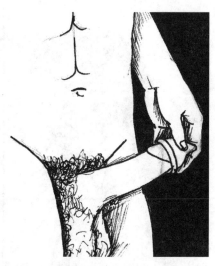

1. Before using the condom, check the
expiration date and package to make
sure there are no tears in the package.
Carefully open package so as not to
tear condom. Check which way condom unrolls. Add lubricant to inside
and outside of condom if desired.

2. Squeeze all of the air out of the tip.
If uncircumsized, pull the foreskin
back before unrolling the condom.

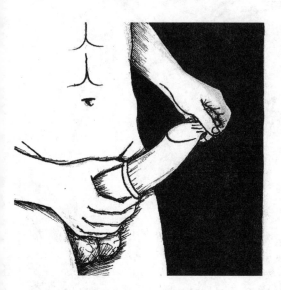

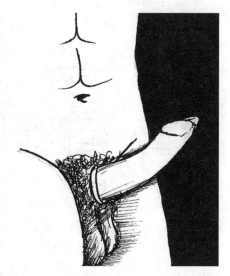

3. While holding the tip with one
hand, unroll the condom with the
other hand on to the penis down to the
base (pubic hair).

4. Have intercourse - periodically check
the condom to make sure it is still in
place and has no tears or breaks.

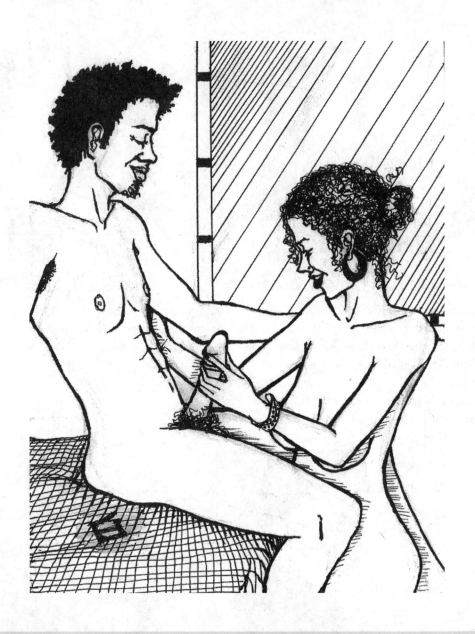

Be Prepared!

My girlfriend and I were talking about having sex, and we both decided we wanted to. One night after a date, we were making out and it reached the point where we both really wanted to have sex. She asked if I had a condom, and I said (very disappointed), "no." I was mad at myself. She whipped one out of her purse. I was surprised that she had one, but very thankful that she was prepared! Jon, 23 years old.

Condoms for Women

Reality female condoms are made of a thin plastic called polyurethane. This is NOT latex or rubber. The condom is placed into the vagina. It is open at one end and closed at the other. Both ends have a flexible ring used to keep the condom in the vagina. The female condom comes in only one size: 15 centimeters in length and 7 centimeters wide. The flexible and removable inner ring at the closed end is inserted into the vagina as far as possible; the inner ring may be removed or left in place in vagina; the larger outer ring remains outside the vagina. Although the female condom has not been tested for effectiveness in infection prevention during anal intercourse, some people choose to use the female condom (without the inner ring) instead of the male condom. Complete information about this contraceptive is available from your clinician, from the package insert, or by calling 1-800-274-6601.

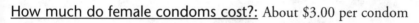

How effective are female condoms?
Perfect user failure rate: **5%**
Typical user failure rate: **21%**
[Source: Trussell, J., Contraceptive Technology, 1998]

How much do female condoms cost?: About $3.00 per condom

What are the advantages of the female condom?
• Gives women a new option in preventing both infection (especially against herpes and HPV, since it covers more of the external genitalia) and pregnancy.
• Gives women more contraceptive control and a sense of freedom.
• An option for a woman who cannot get a man to use a condom.
• Women don't need to see a clinician to get it.
• No prescription or fitting is needed.
• Can be put in up to 8 hours in advance.
• Safe and fairly effective at preventing both pregnancy and infection.
• Your partner can insert it, making it part of sex play.
• Any lubricant may be used with the female condom including oil-based lubricants since this condom is NOT made of latex. It does come with its own lubricant.
• Polyurethane transmits heat well, which may make sex more fun.
• Can be used if either partner is allergic to latex.
• Breakage is rare.

What are the disadvantages of the female condom?
• Less effective than latex male condoms in preventing both pregnancy and STIs.
• Large and some feel it is unattractive or odd-looking. Although it looks different and may appear unusual at first, its size and shape allow it to protect a greater area.

- Some women do not like the idea of putting fingers or a foreign object into their vagina. It is large, bulky, and can be difficult for some women to place into vagina.
- Will not work if the penis enters the vagina outside of the female condom. If this happens, use emergency contraception. Call 1-888-NOT-2-LATE.
- Penis must be directed into the condom.
- Can make rustling noises prior to or during intercourse. The rustling may be due to air. It doesn't always happen. A lubricant may decrease noises if it does occur.
- Not available in as many stores as the male condom. It may be hard to find, so call the store in advance.
- About three times more expensive than a male condom.
- Inner ring may cause discomfort; if it does, it should be removed.

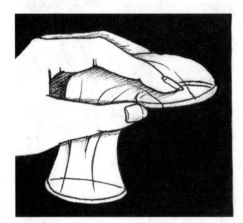 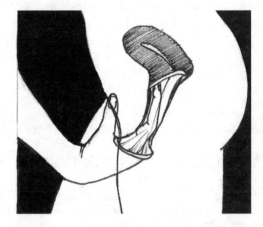

Rustling Female Condom

Some friends of mine were on a road and decided to drop by. After the first night, the girlfriend was really upset because she had forgotten her diaphragm. A couple of months earlier I had obtained some free samples of Reality (the female condom). I was also told two important pieces of information about using Reality: (1) you have to carefully guide the penis so that it does not enter outside of the condom and (2) sometimes, when the penis is (correctly) inside the condom, you might hear a rustling noise. I shared this information with my friend and assured her that I had tried one and it worked well. On their way back from their road trip, they stopped by our place again. Of course, we were curious about how the female condom had worked out for them. They looked at each other and burst out laughing. Apparently, after much adjusting and positioning, she had managed to get the condom in. But, when they heard a rustling noise, they thought it meant they were outside of the condom (which is incorrect) and, nevertheless, kept going. It was then that I realized that, in the heat of the moment, they had confused the two pieces of information. So, remember, always check to make sure the penis is inside the condom and if you hear the rustle you are on the right track! Maxine, 26 years old.

Diaphragm

A diaphragm is a rubber dome-shaped device that a woman places into her vagina so that it covers the cervix, the opening to the uterus. The diaphragm blocks semen from entering the cervix. A spermicide placed onto the diaphragm kills sperm and physically and chemically blocks it from entering the uterus.

How effective is the diaphragm?
Perfect user failure rate: **6%**
Typical user failure rate: **20%**   *[Source: Trussell, J., Contraceptive Technology, 1998]*

How much does the diaphragm cost?: $15-18 plus office visit and spermicide.

What are the advantages of the diaphragm?
• The diaphragm is fairly effective and gives the woman control. When used perfectly, only 6 women in 100 become pregnant the first year using a diaphragm.
• The diaphragm can be put in within 6 hours of initiation of sexual intimacy.
• Your partner can put it in as part of sex play.
• There are no hormones involved, and thus, there are no hormonal side effects.
• The penis can remain inside the vagina after ejaculation.
• Intercourse during a woman's period is less messy. The diaphragm holds back menstrual fluid.
• The diaphragm may slightly reduce the risk for cervical infections, including gonorrhea, chlamydia, human papilloma virus (HPV), and pelvic inflammatory disease (PID).

What are the disadvantages of the diaphragm?
• This method has relatively high failure rates.
• You must be fitted for a diaphragm by a clinician.
• You should wash your hands with soap and water before putting in your diaphragm.
• Insertion of the diaphragm may interrupt sex.
• Using the diaphragm increases your risk for urinary tract infections.
• Some women find the diaphragm unattractive, inconvenient or bulky.
• If you do not like touching your vagina, the diaphragm may not be a good method for you.
• It is difficult for some women to insert a diaphragm correctly.
• If left in too long, the diaphragm slightly increases your risk for a serious infection called toxic shock syndrome. Don't leave your diaphragm in for more than 48 hours.
• The diaphragm may slip out of place during sex. If you change positions, you may want to check to see that the diaphragm is still covering the cervix.
• A new fitting may be necessary after having a baby, an abortion, miscarriage, or gaining 15 pounds.
• The diaphragm must be left in place 6 hours after the last act of intercourse.

How do I use the diaphragm?

1. You must be fitted in a clinician's office for a diaphragm. Be sure you are shown how to insert and remove the diaphragm. You should also walk around your clinician's office to test its long-term comfort.
2. You will be given a prescription for the specific type of diaphragm you will use. You must go to a drugstore to get the actual diaphragm and the spermicide to use with the diaphragm.
3. Insert no longer than 6 hours before intercourse.
4. *To insert:* Fill inner surface of diaphragm 2/3 full with 2 teaspoons of spermicide before insertion. Squeeze the ring together with your thumb and index finger. Insert the diaphragm into your vagina using your index finger. The diaphragm should fit snugly over the cervix.
5. Before each act of intercourse, check to make sure the diaphragm is in place. If you have intercourse again, add more spermicide into the vagina using the applicator that comes with the spermicide. Do not remove the diaphragm to add spermicide.
6. Leave in place for at least 6 hours and no longer than 24 hours after intercourse.
7. Avoid oil-based lubricants or vaginal products such as Vaseline or yeast infection creams because they can break down the latex diaphragm.
8. After removal, clean with soap and water, rinse, dry, and store diaphragm in its case in a cool, clean, dry, and dark area.
9. Check regularly for any stiffness, holes, cracks, or other defects by holding the diaphragm up to light or putting it in water to watch for bubbles.

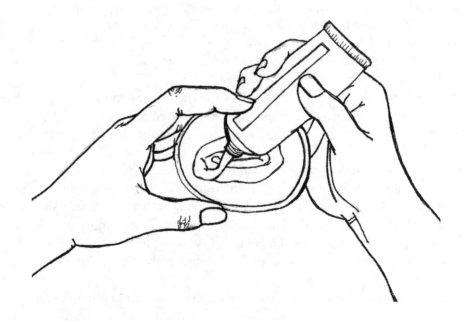

10. Have the diaphragm checked each year by a clinician and replace it every 3 years. Recheck the fit if you have a 20% weight loss or gain or after pregnancy.
11. Drug and alcohol use can reduce the effectiveness of the diaphragm. Being drunk or high increases the risk of making a mistake.
12. If the diaphragm dislodges or is not properly used, use emergency contraception.

The Wrong Kind of Jelly

A woman returned pregnant to our clinic stating she had used her diaphragm each and every time. She claimed she always used jelly in it. But, she was using the wrong kind. Rather than using a spermicidal or other contraceptive jelly she was using Welch's grape jelly. Her diaphragm had an unmistakable purple hue. Sean, clinic nurse.

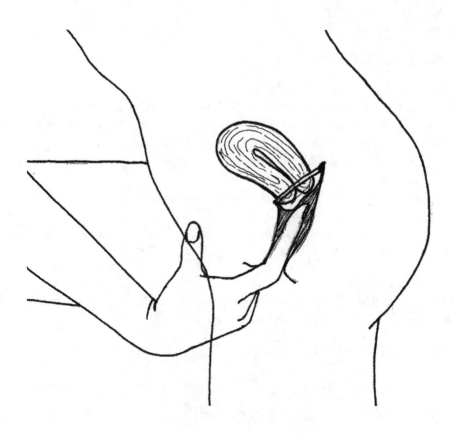

Fertility Awareness Methods

Fertility awareness methods use physical signs, symptoms, and menstrual cycle data to determine when ovulation occurs. During the time of the month when pregnancy is most likely to occur, the couple abstains from sexual intercourse or uses barrier methods. Fertility awareness methods requires careful awareness, planning, and commitment on the part of both partners. It is most effective when the couple has received training on how to use the methods.

Types of fertility awareness methods include:

Calendar Method

This method uses a calendar to track menstrual cycles. Assuming that sperm can live up to 3 days and ovulation occurs 14 days before the first day of menstrual bleeding, fertile periods are calculated based on the time span during which ovulation is expected to occur.

How effective is the calendar method?
Perfect use failure rate: **9%**
Typical use failure rate: **25%**   *[Source: Trussell, J., Contraceptive Technology, 1998]*

How much does the calendar method cost? Free

How do I use the calendar method?
1. Record your menstrual cycles for 6 months prior to starting the method.
2. Find the longest and shortest of your past menstrual cycles. (A cycle begins on day 1 menstrual bleeding and continues until the day before the next bleeding begins.)
3. The earliest day of the fertile period equals the number of days of your shortest cycle minus 18.
4. The latest day of the fertile period equals the number of days of your longest cycle minus 11.
5. During fertile periods, either abstain from vaginal-penile intercourse or use a barrier method.

Cervical Mucus Method

To use this method, a woman checks the quantity and character of the mucus on the vulva or vaginal opening to detect ovulation.

How effective is the cervical mucus method?
Perfect use failure rate: **3%**
Typical use failure rate: **25%**   *[Source: Trussell, J., Contraceptive Technology, 1998]*

How much does the cervical mucus method cost? Free

How do I use the cervical mucus method?

1. Using your finger or a tissue, collect a small amount of mucus from the vaginal opening each day and record the type:
   - *Post-menstrual fertile mucus: scant or undetectable*
   - *Pre-ovulation fertile mucus: cloudy, yellow or white, sticky*
   - *Ovulation mucus: thick, slippery, clear*
   - *Post-ovulation fertile mucus: thin, cloudy, sticky*
   - *Post-ovulation post-fertile mucus: scant or undetectable*
2. When using this method before ovulation, wait 24 hours after intercourse to make the test accurate.
3. Use abstinence or a barrier method during the 4-day fertile period
4. Have intercourse without restriction only during post-ovulatory infertile periods.
5. NOTE: Douching, having a vaginal infection, and using vaginal spermicides will make it difficult to interpret cervical mucus.

Basal Body Temperature (BBT) Method

This method uses a digital thermometer to monitor a woman's body temperature. At ovulation, the temperature will increase noticeably (0.4 – 0.8°F).

How effective is the basal body temperature method?

Perfect use failure rate: **3%**

Typical use failure rate: **25%**   *[Source: Trussell, J., Contraceptive Technology, 1998]*

How much does the basal body temperature method cost?

$5-10 for a BBT thermometer

How do I use the basal body temperature method?

1. Take your temperature daily and record cycles prospectively for 6 months before starting method.
2. The fertile period is defined as the day of the first elevation in temperature through 3 consecutive days of elevated temperature.
3. Abstain or use a barrier method during fertile periods.
4. NOTE: Temperature may not be accurate if a woman is sick and has a fever.

Basal Body Temperature Changes During a Menstrual Cycle

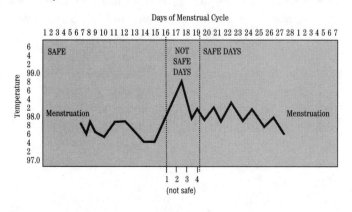

Post-Ovulation and Symptothermal Methods

The post-ovulation method permits intercourse only after signs of ovulation have subsided until menstrual bleeding. This is the **most effective** fertility awareness method.

How effective is the post-ovulation method?
Perfect use failure rate: 1%
Typical user failure rate: 25%   *[Source: Trussell, J., Contraceptive Technology, 1998]*

The symptothermal method combines at least two of the above methods, usually cervical mucus with basal body temperature.

How effective are symptothermal methods?
Perfect use failure rate: 2%
Typical use failure rate: 25%

What are the advantages of fertility awareness methods?
• Helps women learn more about menstrual physiology.
• No side effects or complications from hormones.
• Inexpensive.
• Partners can work together in using this method.
• May be the only method in line with religious beliefs.
• Can be used in reverse to help couples get pregnant.

What are the disadvantages of fertility awareness methods?
• No protection against STIs, including HIV.
• High failure rate for populations of typical users. Excellent record-keeping increase effectiveness. For example, to become a perfect user, a woman must take her BBT every single morning before getting out of bed.
• Works poorly for women who have irregular or unpredictable menstrual cycles
• It takes at least 6 months of recording cycles to learn how to use natural family planning methods. During this time you must abstain or use a barrier method.
• Requires discipline, good communication, and full commitment of both partners.

Contraceptive Implants: Implanon (the single-rod implant)

Implanon consists of a single implant (slightly longer than one Norplant implant) that is inserted under the skin of the upper arm. Implanon contains the hormone, etonogestrel, that is released slowly each day and stays effective for 3 years. Within 24 hours of insertions, thick cervical musus stops sperm from going through the cervix. Implanon also prevents ovulation and makes the lining of the uterus thin. Implanon is now being reviewed by the U.S. Food and Drug Administration and is not yet available in the United States (although it is currently on the market in 9 European countries). Insertion and removal are far easier with Implanon than with Norplant implants, so the popularity of Implanon may be far greater than the popularity of Norplant. I addition, because Norplant is currently unavailable to women in the U.S., Implanon may prove to be an important contraceptive option.

How effective is Implanon?
Perfect use failure rate: 0.05%
Typical use failure rate: 0.05%

How much does Implanon cost?
Unknown; unavailable in U.S.

What are the advantages of Implanon?
• Insertion is more simple than for Norplant
• Very effective. Single decision and procedure may lead to long-term contraception
• In clinical trials, many women have chosen to continue using Implanon
• Reduced risk of ectopic pregnancy
• May reduce cramping or pain during periods or at the time of ovulation
• Headaches may improve
• Low dose of progestin and no estrogen (dose is slightly higher than Norplant, but less than Depo-Provera)
• May be used by some women who cannot take estrogen
• May cause some women to have no periods (which some may see as an advantage)

What are the disadvantages of Implanon?
• Does not protect against sexually transmitted infections, including HIV/AIDS.
• Removal requires a clinic visit, but is rarely difficult
• Irregular bleeding may lead to no periods in 22% of women (which some may see as a disadvantage)
• Headaches are the most common side effect
• Discontinuation (the percentage of women who stopped using Implanon) ranged from 2% to 23% in 2 major studies. In both, the rates of amennorhea (no periods) and prolonged bleeding were the same but the discontinuation rates varied widely

How do I use Implanon?

1. Starting and using the method is similar to Norplant (see p. 88).

NOTE: Irregular bleeding is normal. If your pattern of bleeding is unacceptable, go back to your clinician because there are several things that may make your bleeding pattern more acceptable (e.g., taking a cycle of combined birth control pills). You may not get periods. This is more common in Depo-Provera users and less common in Norplant users, as compared to Implanon users.

Contraceptive Implants: Norplant

Norplant implants are 6 matchstick-size rods inserted into the upper arm. After you are given a local anesthetic, insertion takes about 7 to 10 minutes. Usually it does not hurt. Implants give off very small amounts of a hormone (levonorgestrel) much like the progesterone a woman produces during the last 2 weeks of each monthly cycle. One and two implant systems, which are easier to insert and remove, may be on the way.

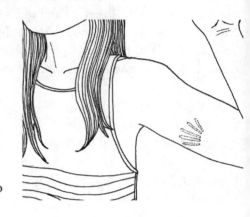

NOTICE: Wyeth-Ayerst, manufacturer of Norplant, recommended that providers discontinue insertion of Norplant from kits distributed beginning October 7, 1999 until further testing can settle questions about their effectiveness. The batches affected by the advisory are from kits with a year 2004 package expiration date. According to the company's Aug. 10, 1999 letter, testing and analysis of the product lots should be completed in about one to two months, with additional information to be provided at that time. In the meantime, all shipments of Norplant have been suspended. It is unknown if or when Norplant will be available again on the market.

How effective are Norplant implants?

Perfect use failure rate: **0.05%**

Typical use failure rate: **0.05%** *[Source: Trussell, J., Contraceptive Technology, 1998]*

How much do Norplant implants cost?

Currently unavailable

*The Norplant Foundation provides free Norplant insertion and help with Norplant removal for women who qualify: 1-800-760-9030.

What are the advantages of Norplant implants?
- Highly effective—only 1 woman in 1,000 becomes pregnant in the first year of Norplant use.
- Nothing to do on a daily basis or at the time of intercourse.
- When you're using Norplant, you only have to make one clinic visit a year for regular checkups.
- Women using Norplant lose less menstrual blood. They also experience less cramping or pain during periods.
- There is a reduced risk of ectopic pregnancy, although ectopic pregnancies in women who use Norplant are rare.
- May make intercourse more enjoyable by reducing fear of pregnancy.

What are the disadvantages of Norplant implants?
- Norplant is unavailable as of June, 2001 and may not ever be reintroduced.
- Norplant implants do not protect you from sexually transmitted infections, including HIV/AIDS. Use a condom if you or your partner may be at risk.
- Norplant is likely to cause irregular periods. If this is bothersome to you, contact your clinician. There are drugs that may give you a more acceptable pattern of bleeding. As time goes on your periods may become more regular.
- You may gain weight, lose hair, develop headaches, or note darkening of the skin over your implants.
- Implants may cause some arm discomfort.
- Depression, anxiety, mood changes, and premenstrual symptoms may improve or become worse.
- A woman may have trouble finding a clinician who will remove her implants.
- You may be able to see the implants under the skin.
- Norplant is less effective if you take drugs that affect the liver (e.g. rifampicin, griseofulvin, and most antiseizure medicines).
- The initial cost for Norplant is high.

How do I use Norplant?
1. When it is available on the market, you can get Norplant implants from your doctor, nurse practitioner, nurse mid-wife, health department, or family planning clinic. Not all clinicians insert implants, so check in advance.
2. Be sure the clinician putting your implants in is experienced at removing implants and will remove them whether or not you are able to pay to have them removed. You will probably be given a date to return about one month after insertion to check out the insertion site and to answer any questions you may have.
3. You may also qualify for free Norplant Implants from the Norplant Foundation. Call 1-800-760-9030 for information. The foundation can also help you get your Norplant removed.
4. After insertion, keep the insertion area dry for 4 days.

5. Bandage wrap may be taken off in 1-2 days, but let the small adhesive bandage fall off on its own.
6. Expect irregular bleeding when using Norplant. If the bleeding pattern is unacceptable to you, go back to your clinician because there are some things that may be done to improve it.
7. Norplant slowly gets less effective after 5 years. If you want to have a new set put in, you can have the first set removed and a new set inserted at the same time. Talk to your clinician.
8. Return to your clinician immediately if you develop any of these warning signs:
   • *Severe lower abdominal pain (possible ectopic pregnancy)*
   • *Very heavy bleeding during your period*
   • *Severe arm pain*
   • *Pus, redness, heat, or bleeding at the insertion site*
   • *Part or all of an implant has been pushed out*
   • *Severe headaches or blurred vision*
   • *Possible pregnancy (missed period, nausea)*

Intrauterine Device (IUD): Copper T 380A (Paragard)

An intrauterine device, or IUD, is a small device that is placed inside the uterus. The vertical and horizontal arms of the Copper T 380A IUD contain copper that is slowly released into the uterine cavity. Copper stops sperm from making their way up through the uterus into the tubes, and it reduces the ability of sperm to fertilize the egg. It also prevents a fertilized egg from successfully implanting in the lining of the uterus if fertilization has occurred.

How effective is the Copper T 380A IUD?
Perfect use failure rate: **0.6%**
Typical use failure rate: **0.8%**

How much does the Copper T 380A IUD cost?
Device   *$100-$200*
Insertion   *$65-$200*
Removal   *$10-$70*

What are the advantages of the Copper T 380A IUD?
• Highly effective
• Effective for at least 12 years.
• Prevents ectopic pregnancies.
• Far more readily reversible than tubal sterilization or vasectomy.
• Very low cost over time.
• Use of an IUD is convenient, safe, and private.
• All you have to do is check for the strings each month.

- May be used by women who cannot use estrogen–containing birth control pills.
- May be inserted immediately following the delivery of a baby or immediately after an abortion.
- Some studies of IUDs have shown a decreased risk for uterine cancer. There is also evidence that IUDs actually protect against cervical cancer.
- Most effective emergency contraceptive option (see page 111).

What are the disadvantages of the Copper T 380A IUD?
- The IUD provides no protection against sexually transmitted infections. Use condoms to decrease this risk of infection.
- There may be cramping, pain or spotting after insertion.
- The number of bleeding days is slightly higher than normal and you may have somewhat increased menstrual cramping. If your bleeding pattern is bothersome to you, contact your clinician. There are medications that may give you a more acceptable pattern of bleeding and cramping.
- There is a high initial cost of insertion. However, after 2 years, it is the most cost-effective method.
- The IUD must be inserted by a doctor, nurse practitioner, nurse midwife or physician's assistant.
- A small percentage of women are allergic to copper.
- Some men can feel the IUD strings during intercourse.

How do I use the Copper T 380-A IUD?
1. You can get an IUD from your doctor, nurse practitioner, nurse midwife or health department. Not all clinicians insert IUDs. Check in advance.
2. Most clinics insert IUDs when a woman has her period or within 7 days after her period starts. If the risk of pregnancy can be excluded it may be possible to insert an IUD at any time in the cycle.
3. If you experience cramps or pain after initial insertion, taking a pain reliever such as ibuprofen can help.
4. Check the IUD strings at least after each monthly period. Frequent checks are important to make sure the IUD is correctly in place.
5. If your bleeding pattern bothers you, contact your clinician. There are medicines you can take that can help improve the bleeding pattern.
6. Return to your clinician immediately if you experience any of the following warning signs:

P	Period late (pregnancy), abnormal spotting or bleeding
A	Abdominal pain, pain with intercourse
I	Infection exposure (any STI), abnormal discharge
N	Not feeling well, fever, chills
S	String missing, shorter, or longer

Levonorgestrel Intrauterine System: Mirena

An intrauterine contraceptive is a small device that is placed inside the uterus. The Food and Drug Administration (FDA) approved Mirena, the levonorgestrel-releasing intrauterine system, in 2000. Mirena is more effective in preventing pregnancy than tubal ligation and lasts for 7-8 years or more. This method has been available for 10 years in Europe and has been used by approximately 2 million women worldwide. The vertical arm of this device contains a hormone called levonorgestrel. Levonorgestrel is a progestin much like the progesterone a woman's ovaries produce each monthly cycle. Each week Mirena gives off about the same amount of levonorgestrel as a woman gets when she takes one or two of the minipills called Ovrette. The levonorgestrel causes the cervical mucus to become thicker so sperm cannot reach the egg.

How effective is Mirena?
Perfect use failure rate: 0.1%
Typical use failure rate: 0.1%   *[Source: Trussell, J., Contraceptive Technology, 1998]*

How much does Mirena cost?
$300-$400

What are the advantages of Mirena?
• The most effective reversible method ever developed.
• Prevents ectopic pregnancies and pelvic inflammatory disease;
• Decreases menstrual cramping and dramatically decreases menstrual blood loss (a 97% reduction in menstrual blood loss in one study). Some women experience an absence of menstrual bleeding after one year.
• May be left in place for at least 5 years (probably effective for 8 or more years).
• Intrauterine contraceptives are safe, inexpensive over time, and provide extremely effective long-term contraception from a single decision. Mirena is the most effective reversible contraceptive ever developed.
• All you have to do is check for the strings each month.
• Once Mirena is removed, fertility returns rapidly.

What are the disadvantages of Mirena?
• Mirena provides no protection against sexually transmitted infections. Use condoms if there is any risk.
• Use of Mirena often changes the menstrual cycle. There may be more bleeding days than normal for the first few months and less than normal after 6 to 8 months. If your bleeding pattern is bothersome, contact your clinician. There are medications that can help you have a better pattern of bleeding.
• High initial cost of insertion.

- Women who have a recent history of pelvic inflammatory disease (PID) are not appropriate candidates. Use of IUDs has been associated with a very slightly increased risk of PID.

How do I use Mirena?
See guidelines for Copper T 380A IUD (page 59).

Progestasert Intrauterine Contraceptive
An intrauterine contraceptive is a small device that is placed inside the uterus. Progestasert device is shaped like a "T" and its vertical arm contains the hormone progesterone. This progesterone is exactly the same as the progesterone a woman's ovaries produce each monthly cycle. Progesterone causes the cervical mucus to become thicker so sperm cannot get to the egg. The progesterone also changes the lining of the uterus so implantation of a fertilized egg cannot occur.

How effective is Progestasert?
Perfect use failure rate: **1.5%**
Typical use failure rate: **2.0%**   *[Source: Trussell, J., Contraceptive Technology, 1998]*

How much does the Progestasert IUD cost?
Device   *$82/year*
Insertion   *$60-$200/year*
Removal   *$10-$70/year*

What are the advantages of Progestasert ?
- Provides effective contraception for one year (approved for 18 months in France).
- Decreased menstrual cramping and menstrual blood loss with use of this IUD.
- There is nothing to do at the time of intercourse.
- IUDs are far more easily reversible than male or female sterilization.
- All you have to do is check for the strings each month.
- This IUD may be used by some women who cannot take estrogen.

What are the disadvantages of Progestasert?
- No protection against sexually transmitted infections, including HIV/AIDS.
- Use of Progestasert commonly leads to irregular periods and increases the number of days some women have spotting. While there is less overall blood loss, the number of bleeding days is greater than normal. If your bleeding pattern is bothersome to you, contact your clinician. There are medications that can give you a more acceptable pattern of bleeding.

- Some women stop having periods completely. If you know that this may happen with Progestasert, you may actually enjoy not having monthly periods.
- There may be some cramping or pain at the time of insertion.
- Progestasert has to be replaced in one year (although it is approved for 18 months in France); other IUDs can be left in longer.
- It is costly to remove and reinsert a new one each year.
- There is a slightly increased risk of pelvic inflammatory disease at the time of insertion.

How do I use Progestasert? See guidelines for Copper T 380A IUD (page 59).

Outercourse
Outercourse, as opposed to intercourse, refers to types of sexual activity that do not involve the penis entering the vagina, mouth, or anus. Some examples include:
- *holding hands*
- *hugs*
- *kisses*
- *touching the genitals or other body parts*
- *mutual masturbation*
- *massaging*
- *fantasizing*

How effective is outercourse?
Unknown; but if used perfectly probably as effective as abstinence.

How much does outercourse cost? Free

What are the advantages of outercourse?
- Outercourse is always an option...there are no supplies needed and it is free!
- It's fun, and there is no worry about pregnancy. For some, it's more fun than penis-vagina intercourse.
- If there is not intercourse—oral, anal, or vaginal—there is some protection, but perhaps not total protection, against sexually transmitted infections.
- There are no medical complications.
- Outercourse can increase emotional closeness between individuals.
- It may be a more acceptable practice for some people's cultures or religions.

What are the disadvantages of outercourse?
- One partner may really want to have intercourse. This can cause stress, and strategies should be discussed to overcome this stress.
- This method may get either partner thinking: "Is this going to go farther than I want?" This concern may decrease their enjoyment.

- A couple may not be prepared to protect themselves from pregnancy or sexually transmitted infections if they switch to intercourse.
- Some sexually transmitted infections can still be transmitted when infected skin touches infected skin (e.g., herpes, HPV).

How do I use outercourse?
1. Start by talking openly with your partner about your sexual limits.
2. Decide in advance how far you may be willing to go (or would like to go) and what you definitely don't want to do.
3. Communicate during sexual activity about your feelings and limits.
4. Remember that some STIs can still be transmitted when infected skin touches infected skin (e.g., herpes, HPV). Talk to your partner about sexual histories!
5. Make a plan for what you will do if you decide to have intercourse—what contraceptive/safer sex method will you use? How will you (or your partner) get it?
6. Use emergency contraception within 72 hours if you decide to have intercourse and do not use protection, if you experience a condom break or slip, or if you are forced to have intercourse.

Birth Control Pills: Combined Estrogen and Progestin

Combined birth control pills contain two hormones, an estrogen and a progestin. They work by stopping ovulation (release of an egg), thickening cervical mucus, and by making the lining of the uterus thinner, thus preventing implantation. A woman takes one pill every day at the same time. Most brands have a 7-day cycle of placebo, or sugar, pills, during which a woman takes pills without hormones and experiences withdrawal bleeding. One brand, Mircette, has only two days of placebo pills.

How effective are combined birth control pills?
Perfect use failure rate: **0.1%**
Typical use failure rate: **5%**
[Source: Trussell, J., Contraceptive Technology, 1998]

How much do combined birth control pills cost?

$14 - $45/pack plus office visit

What are the advantages of combined birth control pills?

- Pills decrease women's menstrual cramps and pain.
- They reduce menstrual blood loss and a woman's risk for anemia.
- Pills decrease a woman's risk for cancer of the ovary and cancer of the lining of the uterus (endometrial cancer). The protective effects of pills against ovarian cancer last for at least 30 years after a woman stops taking pills

- They also lower your chances of having benign breast masses (breast masses which are NOT cancer), ovarian cysts, ectopic pregnancy, and pelvic inflammatory disease (PID).
- Acne often improves, and hair growth on the face is reduced.
- Many women enjoy sex more when on pills because they know they are less likely to get pregnant.
- Some clinicians will provide 3 to 6 months of pills without a pelvic exam.
- You can control the cycle so as not to have your period during certain times (honeymoon, exams, athletic events).
- You can decrease the number of cycles over time (taking 3 series of 21 active pills followed by a pill-free interval of 4 days).

What are the disadvantages of combined birth control pills?
- Pills do not protect you from HIV or other infections. Use a condom if you may be at risk.
- You have to remember to take the pill every day.
- You may have nausea and/or spotting mostly during the first few cycles on pills.
- Pills tend to make periods very short and scanty. You may see no blood at all. Most women like this when they understand it is normal.
- Taking the pill may cause headaches, depression, anxiety, fatigue, mood changes, or decreased enjoyment of sex in some women.
- A backup contraceptive is required for 7 days weeks if you have any question about how many pills you have missed and whether a backup is necessary.
- Serious complications such as blood clots may occur but are incredibly rare.
- Pills can be quite expensive and require a prescription.
- The most recent research shows that young women who have not given birth and are taking combined pills are slightly more likely than those who are not taking pills to be diagnosed with breast cancer - about 1 in 1000 women under the age of 45. This may be because pills promote the growth of exising breast cancer or because women who use pills are more likley to get an exam and then be diagnosed. Breast cancers diagnosed while taking pills and in the years after a woman stops taking pills are less likely to spread to other parts of the body. Women who have taken pills and are over 45 years old are at no increased risk of having breast cancer diagnosed.
They may lead to higher rates of one type of cervical cancer (adenocarcinoma of the cervix).
- After stopping pills, you may not get your period for 1-3 months.
- You cannot take pills if you smoke or are over 35.

How do I use combined pills?

1. In the United States you need a prescription. You can get pills from your doctor, nurse practitioner, nurse midwife, health department, or family planning clinic.
2. Use a backup contraceptive for the first 7 days of your first pack of pills.
3. You do not need to use a backup method during the hormone-free days of your pill pack.
4. Take one pill a day at the same time. Try to incorporate taking your pills with another regular, daily activity such as brushing your teeth to make sure you take the pills as part of a routine.
5. Nausea and spotting (slight bleeding) are most common in the first few months of pill use
6. You will need to have regular check-ups by your clinician once you start taking pills.
7. Drugs or alcohol use can reduce the effectiveness of pills. For example, being drunk or high may increase the risk of missing a pill.
8. If you miss one pill, take the missed pill as soon as you remember. Take the next pill on schedule. You can use emergency contraception or a backup method for the week after one missed pill if you want to do everything you can to minimize your risk for unintended pregnancy.
9. If you miss two pills, take the missed pills as soon as you remember. If missed pills were anytime in the first week of the cycle, strongly consider emergency contraception if you have had sex without a backup method. Take the next pill on schedule and use backup contraception for 7 days. If the missed pills were later than the first week of a new pack, consider emergency contraception if you have had sex without a backup method. Take next pill on schedule and use a backup contraceptive for the next 7 days. Remember that two missed pills may cause spotting in a few days. DO NOT STOP taking pills. Continue on schedule.
10. Contact your clinician immediately if you have any of these warning signs:

A	Abdominal pain? Yellow skin or eyes?
C	Chest pain?
H	Headaches that are severe?
E	Eye problems? Blurred vision or loss of vision
S	Severe leg pain or swelling in the calf or thigh?

Birth Control Pills: Progestin-Only

Progestin-only pills contain just one hormone, a progestin. A cycle does not have hormone-free days (placebo pills). Progestin-only pills work by making cervical mucus thicker so sperm cannot reach the egg, and by making the lining of the uterus thinner. Sometimes they stop ovulation (release of an egg).

How effective are progestin-only pills?
Perfect use failure rate: **0.5%**
Typical use failure rate: **5%**   *[Source: Trussell, J., Contraceptive Technology, 1998]*

How much do progestin-only pills cost?
$17-$30/pack plus office visit.

What are the advantages of progestin-only pills?
• There are no estrogen side effects. Progestin-only pills can be taken by women who have had side effects or complications using combined pills.
• The amount of the progestin in progestin-only is less than in combined pills.
• Progestin-only pills may be less confusing to take than combined pills. You take exactly the same kind of pill every single day.
• There are decreased cramps and pain during periods, including problems that other treatments have not been able to help.
• There is also decreased pain at the time of ovulation in some women.
• Progestin-only pills can be taken by women who have had thrombophlebitis (inflamed veins).
• They can be taken by women who smoke and are over 35 years of age whereas women who take combined pills cannot.
• Women on mini-pills often experience fewer headaches than those on combined pills.

What are the disadvantages of progestin-only pills?
• Progestin-only pills do not protect you from HIV or other sexually transmitted infections. Use a condom to reduce your risk of infection.
• Menstrual irregularity is the most common problem with progestin-only pills. While the amount of blood lost is less, bleeding may be at irregular intervals and there may be spotting between periods.
• Progestin-only pills tend to make periods very short and scanty. You may go several months with no bleeding at all. (However, some women go years without a period and love it!)
• You have to remember to take a pill every single day at the same time. Staying on schedule is important because progestin-only pills cause cervical mucus to thicken for only 24 hours.

- The failure rate with progestin-only pills is a bit higher in perfect users than the perfect-user failure rate with regular birth control pills (combined pills).
- Some women use a backup method such as condoms as long as they are on progestin-only pills.
- Some pharmacies may not carry progestin-only pills. You should call in advance to find out if they carry them.

How do I use progestin-only pills?

1. In the United States you need a prescription. You can get pills from your doctor, nurse practitioner, nurse midwife, health department, or family planning clinic.
2. Use a backup contraceptive for the first 2 week of your first pack of pills.
3. You do not need to use a backup method during the hormone-free days of your pill pack.
4. Take one pill a day at the same time. Try to incorporate taking your pills with another regular, daily activity such as brushing your teeth. **It is critical to take your pill at the same time each day because progestin-only pills cause cervical mucus to thicken for only 24 hours.**
5. You will need to have regular check-ups by your clinician once you start taking pills.
6. Drugs or alcohol use can reduce the effectiveness of pills. For example, being drunk or high may increase the risk of missing a pill.
7. If you miss a pill, take the missed pill as soon as you remember. Take the next pill on schedule. Use backup contraception for the next 7 days. You can use emergency contraception or a backup method for the week after one missed pill if you want to do everything you can to minimize your risk for unintended pregnancy.
8. Contact your clinician immediately if you:
   - *Miss any periods or have any signs of pregnancy*
   - *Have irregular or heavy bleeding*
   - *Have headaches or vision problems*

Birth Control Shots - Depo-Provera, The Every-Three-Months Progestin Only Injectable

Two "birth control shots," or injectables, are available to women - Depo-Provera and Lunelle. Depo-Provera, is administered once every three months. It provides a hormone much like the progesterone a woman produces during the last 2 weeks of each monthly cycle. It stops the woman from releasing an egg and provides other contraceptive effects. Many clinics recommend that you use a backup contraceptive for a week after your first shot.

How effective is Depo Provera?

Perfect user failure rate:
Less than 0.3%
Typical user failure rate: 0.3%
[Source: Trussell, J., Contraceptive Technology, 1998]

How much does Depo-Provera cost?

$30 per injection plus office visit (may be less expensive on college campuses).

What are the advantages of Depo-Provera shots?
- Nothing must be taken daily or used at the time of sexual intercourse.
- Sex may be enjoyed more because of less fear of pregnancy.
- Depo-Provera is extremely effective. If women receive their injections right on time (every 3 months or 13 weeks), only 3 women in 1,000 will become pregnant in the course of one year.
- Women lose less blood using Depo-Provera and have less menstrual cramping. Often after 3 injections women stop having periods, which is safe!
- Privacy is a major advantage. No one has to know you are using this method.
- Depo-Provera may reduce common symptoms associated with PMS, menstrual cramps, depression and endometriosis. Can prevent ectopic pregnancies.
- Unlike combined pills, Depo-Provera is not less effective if you take medicines that affect the liver.

What are the disadvantages of Depo Provera shots?
- Depo-Provera does not protect you from HIV or other infections. Use condoms to reduce your risk of infection
- Depo-Provera injections can lead to very irregular periods. If your bleeding pattern is bothersome to you, you can take medications, which may give you a more acceptable pattern of bleeding.
- Some women gain weight. To avoid weight gain, watch your calories and exercise regularly.
- You must return to the clinic every three months for your injection.
- Depression and premenstrual symptoms may become worse.
- It may be a number of months before your periods return to normal after your last shot. It takes an average of 10 months for fertility to return after the last shot, making it hard to plan pregnancy exactly.

- Depo-Provera may lower your estrogen level and contribute to bone loss, although this is not certain. Get regular exercise and take extra calcium to protect your bones from osteoporosis.
- A few women are allergic to Depo-Provera. Fortunately, allergic reactions are very rare, but they occur, and the effects of the shot cannot be stopped once it is given. Such a woman may need anti-allergy medicine.
- Depo-Provera is expensive in some healthcare settings.
- Depo-Provera has been associated with an increase in LDL (bad cholesterol) and decrease in HDL (good cholesterol) in some studies.

How do I use Depo-Provera?
1. You can get Depo-Provera injections from your campus health center, clinician, health department, or family planning clinic.
2. Most clinics provide the first shot when a woman has her period or within 7 days after the start of her period.
3. Be sure to return on time for your next shot or you risk decreasing the effectiveness.

Birth Control Shots: Lunelle, the Once-A-Month Combined Injectable
The FDA recently has approved another type of birth control shot called Lunelle. Lunelle contains both estrogen and progestin and is administered once a month.

How effective is Lunelle?
Perfect use failure rate: **0.2 - 0.4%**
Typical use failure rate: **Same**

How much does Lunelle cost?
The cost of Lunelle is still being determined. The price of a dose to a private doctor is $20 and injections are being administered to patients for $7-$20 (with an average of $15/injection). Thus, women are paying about $35/month (injection plus dose of Lunelle) for Lunelle from private doctors. Public sector clinics are paying between $12-$17 per dose and may charge nothing or somewhat more for injection plus a dose of Lunelle.

What are the advantages of Lunelle?
- A woman is more likely to have a very regular bleeding pattern. (More regular than women on no hormonal contraceptive and much more regular than on a progestin-only method such as Depo-Provera).
- Single shot gives 1 month of contraception. Excellent method for women who have difficulty remembering to take pills every single day.
- Nothing to do at the time of intercourse.

- Private and confidential.
- Fertility returns quickly (average of 2 months).
- Highly effective.
- Method is somewhat forgiving of women who do not make it back in 28 days for next shot. Shots may be given after 28 plus or minus 5 days. In other words, a follow-up shot may be given 23 to 33 days after the last shot.

What are the disadvantages of Lunelle?
- No protecion against sexually transmitted infections, including HIV.
- Possible irregular periods (less than with Depo-Provera).
- Must return to clinic every month for an injection.
- You may not like repeated injections.
- Medicine cannot be reveresed once shot is given.
- Can be expensive in some clinics.
- May cause breast tenderness.

How do I use Lunelle?
1. You can get Lunelle injections from your campus health center, clinician, health department, or family planning clinic.
2. Most clinics will provide the first shot when a woman has her period or within 7 days after the start of her period.
3. Be sure to return on time for your next shot or you may risk decreasing the effectiveness (see last bullet of "advantages" above).

Spermicides: Film, Foam, Gel, Suppositories, Tablets, and Sponge
In the U.S., nonoxynol-9 (N-9) is the chemical used in spermicide. Spermicides come in the form of vaginal creams, films, foams, gels, suppositories, tablets, and sponges. As barriers, they block sperm from entering the cervix. As chemicals, they attack the tail and body of the sperm, both reducing mobility and decreasing nourishment.

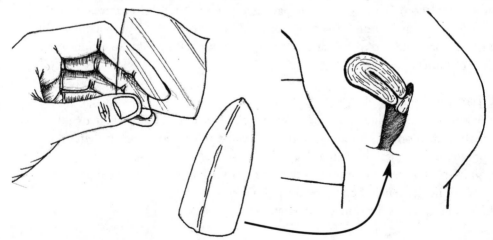

How effective are spermicides?

Perfect use failure rate: **6%**

Typical use failure rate: **26%**

[Source: Trussell, J., Contraceptive Technology, 1998]

How much do spermicides cost?

On average:

Creams/gels	*$10.00 for 8 ounces*
Film	*$12.00 for 12*
Foam	*$11.00 for 0.6 ounces*
Suppositories/tabs	*$13.00 for 18 inserts*

What are the advantages of spermicides?

• No hormonal side effects.
• Lubrication, in the case of foam, may heighten
  sexual pleasure.
• Ease in applying (for some) before or during intercourse.
• Either partner can purchase and apply.
• May be used by woman without partner knowing.
• Possible decrease in HPV transmission may reduce risk of cervical cancer.
• Available over the counter.
• Inexpensive.
• Serves as an immediate back-up if condom should slip or break.

What are the disadvantages of spermicides?

• No protection against HIV/AIDS.
• Minimal, if any, protection against other STIs.
• Possible vaginal, oral, or anal irritation can interrupt sex.
• Taste may be unpleasant.
• At least one partner must feel comfortable inserting fingers into the vagina.
• Some methods (foam) become messy during intercourse.
• Offers none of the potential benefits of hormonal contraception.
• Either partner may have an allergy or be irritated by the chemicals in spermicide.
• Research has indicated that some spermicides (specifically Nonoxynol 9) both
  alone and in conjunction with sponges, diagphragms, and cervical caps, cause
  vaginal irritation and minor ulcerations ni the vaginal lining. The degree of
  inflammation and irritation depends a lot on the frequency of intercourse.

How do I use spermidices?

1. Keep spermicides in cool dry places.
2. Before and after applying spermicide, wash and dry your hands.

3. Spermicide should not be expired and package should have no defects.

4. Spermicide is most effective near the cervical opening.

5. Use more spermicide for each act of intercourse.

6. Although the authors do not recommend douching because it can irritate the vaginal lining and make it more susceptible to infection, douching within 6 hours after insertion or after intercourse makes spermicides less effective. If you choose to douche you must wait at least 6 hours after intercourse or be sure to reapply spermicide before next intercourse.
makes spermicides less effective; reapply before next intercourse

7. Drugs and alcohol can greatly reduce the effectiveness of spermicides. Being drunk or high increases the risk of making a mistake.

8. *Creams/foams/gels:* Apply less than 1 hour before intercourse. May drip out of vagina if inserted more than 1 hour before. With foam, shake canister vigorously. Fill plastic applicator with spermicide. Insert applicator deeply into vagina and push plunger (similar to tampon insertion).

9. *Film/suppositories/tablets:* Insert less than 1 hour, but at least 15 minutes before intercourse. With film, fold the sheet in half and then half again. Using fingers or an applicator, place the spermicide suppository, tablet, or folded film deeply in the vagina, as near to the cervix as possible.

10. *Sponge:* Insert the sponge into the vagina up to 2 hours before intercourse. Leave in place for at least 6-8 hours and no longer than 12 hours after sex. Do not leave the sponge in the vagina for more than 24 hours total. This can increase your risk of toxic shock syndrome. Remove the sponge by pulling on the attached ribbon. Discard sponge after use. NOTE: The sponge was taken off the market in 1995 because the company that produced it decided it was too costly to update its manufacturing facility. The FDA is in the process of approving a new manufacturing company and facility. Once this process is complete, the sponge will be available on the U.S. market again.

Female Sterilization: Tubal Sterilization

Tubal sterilization is an operation which blocks the tubes carrying a woman's egg to her uterus. It is the most commonly used method of birth control worldwide. Often the operation is accomplished through an instrument called a laparoscope. This instrument is inserted through a small incision in the abdomen. The tubes are visualized so the surgeon can place rings, apply clips, or cauterize (burn) the tubes. After this operation your eggs will have no way to get to your uterus (the unused eggs are absorbed into the body), and the man's sperm will have no way to get to your egg. The effectiveness of tubal sterilization differs by the method of sterilization and by the woman's age. This operation should be considered permanent. You must be certain you do not want to deliver more children and will not change your mind.

How effective is tubal ligation?

0.8%-3.7% depending on method and timing

[Source: Trussell, J., Contraceptive Technology, 1998]

How much does tubal ligation cost?

$1200-$2500

What are the advantages of tubal ligation?

• A fairly simple operation that is safe and permanent.
• Nothing needs to be done at the time of intercourse.
• There is nothing to remember on a daily basis.
• There are no hormones and no creams or foams involved.
• Tubal sterilization will not affect your sex drive or ability to enjoy sex.
• It is cost-effective in the long run.
• This procedure may help protect against ovarian cancer.

What are the disadvantages of tubal ligation?

• Sterilization will not protect you from HIV or other sexually transmitted infections. Use a condom to reduce your risk of infection.
• Tubal sterilization requires surgery.
• There is some pain or discomfort for several days after the operation. It is better to have someone accompany you on the day of surgery.
• There is no easy way to check after tubal sterilization to see if it is "still working."
• Tubal sterilization is very effective but definitely not 100% effective. The failure rate is as high as 1-5% in the 10 years after the operation. If you think that you are pregnant at any time in the future, return to the clinic immediately.
• Should a pregnancy occur, there is an increased chance that it will be outside of your uterus (an ectopic pregnancy).
• It is difficult to reverse this operation if you later want to become pregnant. The operation to reverse tubal sterilization is highly technical, expensive, and its results cannot be guaranteed. Most insurance companies will not pay for reversal.
• Regret after tubal sterilization is greater if a woman is under 25 when her operation is done, if she divorces or remarries, if a child dies, or if a woman has just had a baby or abortion when she has the operation.
• In most states, a consent form and a 30-day waiting period are required before the procedure can be scheduled.

How do I get a tubal ligation?

1. Some clinicians perform this operation; others do not. You can get a referral to a clinician who does the tubal sterilization operation from your primary care clinician, health department, family planning clinic or local medical society. You can also call the national organization involved in sterilization training and service (Engender Health) at 212-561-8000.
2. You will need to give informed consent. It is a very good idea to involve your partner (if you have one) in the decision and the office visit when you formally consent to the procedure.
3. Remember that regret after tubal sterilization is greater if a woman is under 25 when her operation is done, if she divorces or remarries, if a child dies, or if a woman has just had a baby or abortion when she has the operation.
4. You can get a tubal ligation at any time in your cycle if you are certain you are not pregnant. It is also possible to have the procedure done immediately after birth.

Male Sterilization: Vasectomy

Vasectomy, or male sterilization, is an operation that blocks the tubes, or vas deferens, which carry a man's sperm outside of the body. It is performed in an office or clinic and involves cutting and tying off or cauterizing (burning) the vas deferens—the tubes that transport sperm from the testicles. This operation should be considered permanent. You must be certain you want no more children and will not change your mind.

How effective is vasectomy?
Perfect use failure rate: **0.1%**
Typical use failure rate: **unknown**   *[Source: Trussell, J., Contraceptive Technology, 1998]*

How much does vasectomy cost?
$350-$750

What are the advantages of vasectomy?
- A vasectomy is a minor operation.
- Safe, extremely effective, and permanent.
- Excellent for men who have had all the children they want.
- A vasectomy is less expensive and causes fewer complications than tubal sterilization.
- Any time, even years later, you can have your semen checked to confirm the effectiveness of the vasectomy. If your semen has no sperm, your operation is effective. Used in this manner, vasectomy can be virtually 100% effective.

- A vasectomy gives the man the opportunity to play a responsible role in the contraceptive process.
- It does not affect a man's ability to have an erection, ejaculate, or enjoy sexual activity.

What are the disadvantages of vasectomy?
- Vasectomy provides no protection against sexually transmitted infections including HIV/AIDS.
- A vasectomy requires surgery. Some men are afraid of having an operation near their genitals.
- Some men fear the operation will affect their ability to have intercourse or will interfere with erection.
- There is some pain or discomfort and scrotal discoloring (usually not severe) for several days after the operation. Pain can usually be relieved with mild pain medications.
- The operation is not effective immediately. You will need to use condoms until the sperm clears from the tubes (15-20 ejaculations).
- To find out if you are sterile, have your semen examined under a microscope after about 15 ejaculations.
- Regret after vasectomy is greater if the man's partner is under 25, if he divorces or remarries, if a child dies, or when the vasectomy is done immediately after a new baby.
- The operation to reverse a vasectomy does not always work. It is highly technical, expensive, and its results cannot be guaranteed.

How do I get a vasectomy?
1. You will need to have a general physical exam and go over your medical history with your clinician.
2. You will need to give informed consent.
3. Understand that the method is permanent.
4. After vasectomy, you will have to abstain from intercourse or use backup contraception the next 20 times you ejaculate or for 3 months. Do not consider vasectomy effective until it is confirmed that no sperm are present (has to be confirmed under a microscope at a follow-up visit).

Withdrawal
Also called *coitus interruptus*, withdrawal involves removing the penis immediately prior to ejaculation.

How effective is withdrawal?
Perfect use failure rate: **4%**
Typical use failure rate: **19%**   *[Source: Trussell, J., Contraceptive Technology, 1998]*

How much does withdrawal cost?: Free

What are the advantages of withdrawal?
• No side effects from hormones.
• No barrier methods are needed and abstinence is avoided.
• Readily available method, which encourages male involvement.
• May introduce variety into sexual relationship.
• May increase spontaneity of sex.
• After practice, may increase a man's understanding and awareness of his sexual response cycle.
• Surprisingly effective if used perfectly.

What are the disadvantages of withdrawal?
• Relatively high failure rate among typical users.
• Inadequate protection against sexually transmitted infections, including HIV/AIDS.
• None of the potential benefits from hormonal methods.
• Individuals with early or unpredictable ejaculation may not be able to use.
• Man's instruction and cooperation is needed; requires a great deal of trust.
• May reduce sexual pleasure of man and/or his partner.
• Encourages "spectatoring," or observing and analyzing what is happening during sex.
• Increased fear of pregnancy and infection may decrease enjoyment of sex.

How do I use withdrawal?
1. Practice withdrawal using a backup method, until both partners master the technique.
2. Wipe penis clean of pre-ejaculatory fluid before intercourse.
3. Use sexual positions that reduce deep penetration (e.g., male putting penis in part way in the male-on-top position, female-on-top position, or side-by-side).
4. Right before ejaculation, remove the penis and make sure no ejaculate comes into contact with the vagina or is left around the vaginal opening.
5. Remember that drugs and alcohol can greatly reduce the effectiveness of withdrawal. Being drunk or high increases the risk of making a mistake.
6. Use emergency contraception if you think withdrawal might have failed. Couples using withdrawal would be wise to have emergency contraceptive pills available in advance in case of failure to withdraw in time.

CHAPTER 6:
If Contraception Fails or Isn't Used

Every time intercourse occurs there is a chance of, among other things, pregnancy, pleasure, sexually transmitted infections, or intimacy. Some or all of these may happen and there are various things we can do to try to build these elements into intercourse or try to eliminate them from intercourse. But, let's say for a moment that you did everything perfectly. You weren't drunk. You weren't high. You didn't use Vaseline on the condom. You took the pill at the correct time. Still, something went wrong...

If contraception fails, what will you do? Do you involve the help of your partner? What are your first steps? What choices do you have? The following chapter will help you sort through your options, the time frame within which you will need to act, and, hopefully, will help you make the choice that is best for you.

Emergency Contraception
• Had intercourse unexpectedly?
• Been forced to have sex?
• Had a condom break, slip or come off?
• Forgot to take several birth control pills?
• Got drunk and had sex without protection?
• Expected your partner to pull out... but he didn't?
• Found out after sex your diaphragm had slipped?
• Unintentionally let "outercourse" lead to intercourse without proper protection?

If you answered "yes" to any of these questions, the information in this section may be extremely important for you to know. Emergency contraception is pregnancy prevention after unprotected sex, suspected contraceptive failure, or rape. Emergency contraception is <u>not</u> the "abortion pill" and does not cause an abortion. Rather, it helps <u>prevent</u> unintended pregnancy. There are several methods of emergency contraception: progestin-only pills, combined estrogen/progestin pills, and IUD insertion.

She Missed Her Period

My girlfriend and I have been having sex for a while. Recently, when she missed her period we were both scared that she may be pregnant. We did a home pregnancy test and were so nervous the whole time. We both agree now that we need a back-up method besides condoms. Kenneth, 24 years old.

No Intercourse, But Still Scared

I was with this girl for 2 months and we decided to abstain. We decided that making out in our underwear was as far as we would go. One time I unexpectedly ejaculated early. We weren't sure if any sperm got through her underwear. For a while, she thought she was pregnant. When she finally got her period, we were both relieved, but now we are extra cautious. Will, 20 years old.

Where Am I? What Did I Do?

Once I got drunk at a fraternity party. I was so gone that I didn't remember how I got into this guy's bed. I woke up the next morning, vaguely aware that I had had sex with him. I was so embarrassed and mortified. I did not even know him that well. I am always careful now when I drink. Luckily, I did not get pregnant, because I do not think I could have gotten an abortion. Patria, 21 years old

Emergency Contraceptive Pills (ECPs)

Emergency contraceptive pills (ECPs) are two large doses of ordinary birth pills that may be taken within 72 hours after unprotected intercourse to prevent pregnancy from occurring. Currently, ECPs are available as progestin-only or combined estrogen/progestin and, in all but one state (Washington), a woman must have a prescription in order to get ECPs.

Progestin-only pills (POPs):

Progestin-only ECPs are more effective than combined ECPs. They have a failure rate of 1.1% (compared to 3.2% for combined ECPs), cause less nausea and vomiting than combined ECPs, and are the least expensive emergency contraceptive option. It used to be that a woman had to take a very large number of the pill Ovrette as emergency contraception (20 pills followed by 20 pills, 12 hours later). Now, all the hormones are available in a product called PLAN B, for which a woman takes one pill followed by one pill 12 hours later.

How do I use progestin-only emergency contraception?

PLAN B: Take 1 pill as soon as possible within 72 hours of unprotected intercourse and 1 pill 12 hours later.

Ovrette: Take 20 pills as soon as possible within 72 hours of unprotected intercourse and then 20 pills 12 hours later per dose.

Combined oral contraceptives (COCs):

Combined ECPs have both estrogen and progestin. They have a higher failure rate than progestin-only ECPs (3.2%) and tend to cause more nausea and vomiting than progestin-only ECPs. It used to be that a woman had to take a large number of ordinary combined pills (such as Lo-Ovral or TriPhasil) as emergency contraception. Now, all the hormones are available in a product called PREVEN, for which a woman takes 2 pills followed by 2 pills 12 hours later.

How do I use combined emergency contraception?

Preven: Take 2 pills as soon as possible within 72 hours of unprotected intercourse, and 2 more pills 12 hours later.

Ovral: Take 2 pills as soon as possible within 72 hours of unprotected intercourse and then 2 more pills 12 hours later.

Levlen,
Lo-Ovral, Take 4 pills as soon as possible within 72 hours of unprotected intercourse
Nordette, or and 4 more pills 12 hours later.
TriPhasil:

Alesse: Take 5 pills as soon as possible within 72 hours of unprotected intercourse, and 5 more pills 12 hours later.

Where can I get emergency contraception pills?

You can go to your campus health center, clinician, or family planning clinic to obtain ECPs. Some clinicians are not familiar with emergency contraception. In this case, call the toll-free hotline, 1-800-584-9911 or 1-888-NOT-2-LATE for phone numbers of clinicians near you who prescribe emergency contraceptive pills. This hotline provides information about other emergency contraceptive options. Some of these sources of help are free. You can also go to these websites for additional information: www.opr.princeton.edu, www.PREVEN.com, or www.go2planB.com. PLAN B is the emergency contraceptive pill that causes the least nausea, the least vomiting, and is most effective.

My Boyfriend Told Me About Emergency Contraception

I was having sex with my boyfriend. We had used a condom as usual, but I noticed a tear in the latex after he withdrew. I felt a sudden sense of panic, even though my boyfriend was trying to reassure me that there were some "morning after" pills I could get at a local clinic. The rest of the night I spent tossing and turning. In the morning, my boyfriend walked with me over to the clinic in town. The clinician prescribed the appropriate pills. While I felt slight nausea and discomfort, I also felt a sense of relief. I had always practiced safer sex and was by no means ready at that tender age of 22 to have a child of my own. Korina, 22 years old.

Mutual Responsibility

I am a 19-year-old sophomore in college. My first sexual experience quickly ended when the condom broke. My boyfriend went with me to the doctor's office where I was given emergency contraception (the "morning after pill"). Although my first sexual experience was not wonderful in the physical sense, it was wonderful in another way. My boyfriend's concern for me brought us closer together and made our relationship stronger. I am VERY thankful for modern technology. I don't know what I would have done if I had gotten pregnant during college. Jo, 19 years old.

IUD Insertion

For up to 5 to 8 days after unprotected intercourse, you can have an intrauterine device (IUD) inserted to keep you from getting pregnant. This is the most effective currently available postcoital contraceptive in the United States. The failure rate is 0.1%. When used after unprotected intercourse, the Copper T 380 A IUD is inserted into the uterus. It prevents implantation of a fertilized egg (if an egg was fertilized by the unprotected sex). Women wanting the most effective emergency contraceptive should consider IUD insertion. It has about one-tenth the failure rate of pills.

Where can I get an IUD inserted after unprotected sex?

You can go to your campus health center clinician or family planning clinic. Some clinicians are not familiar with emergency contraception. In this case, call the toll-free hotline: 1-888-NOT-2-LATE to obtain the phone numbers of clinicians near you who can insert an emergency IUD. Some of these sources of help are free. You also can go to www.opr.princeton.edu for additional information.

Pregnancy Options

If you are pregnant and did not plan to be pregnant, you have a very important decision to make. It may be a difficult decision. Speak to your clinician or family planning clinic staff about your concerns. If you choose to continue with your pregnancy, stop drinking, smoking, or using other drugs immediately and start seeing a physician or nurse midwife right away. You may choose to raise the baby yourself (or with help from your partner or family members) or you may choose to place the baby up for adoption. If you choose to have an abortion, talk to your clinician about where you can have it done safely. The earlier in pregnancy an abortion is done, the safer and less expensive it is for you. You should decide to do what you feel is right. You may want to discuss this decision with your partner, counselor, friend, religious leader, or family member. Or you may want to keep this decision to yourself. The authors believe that none of these options is always right or always wrong. The best choice is the one you make for yourself.

Finally, there may come a time in your life when you want and plan to have children. We hope you are able to make this decision just that—a decision.

Signs of Pregnancy

It is necessary to be familiar with signs of pregnancy. Unfortunately, symptoms also can exist without being pregnant. It is best to see a clinician in order to get a pregnancy test.

Some signs of pregnancy are:
• A missed period
• Breast tenderness and nipple sensitivity
• Fatigue
• Nausea
• Vomiting
• Urinary frequency
• Increased appetite
• Abnormal bleeding or spotting
• Abdominal pain
• Weight gain

As I Planned It...

When I was 29 years old, my partner of 6 years, Philip, and I became pregnant. We had been trying for a year and were thrilled to hear from my doctor that the pregnancy test was positive. Being pregnant was one of the most special times in my life, especially sharing the experience with Philip. It has brought us closer in so many ways and we eagerly await the arrival of our new family member. Tashi, 29.

Carrying pregnancy to term

If you choose to carry the pregnancy to term, there are some things you need to know and do to help ensure a safe pregnancy and healthy infant.

- STOP DRINKING alcoholic beverages. Even small amounts are dangerous for your baby. Avoid alcohol tonight and for the rest of this pregnancy! Fetal alcohol syndrome is the most common known cause of mental retardation. Just one drink a day puts your baby at increased risk for a number of major and minor problems.
- TAKE FOLIC ACID. Go to your local drug store today and tell them you need prenatal vitamins with at least 0.4 milligrams of folic acid per day. Folic acid helps prevent some types of severe birth defects like spinal bifida and congenital heart defects. Even if you are not pregnant now, but may be considering pregnancy in the future, start taking folic acid now. This is an important vitamin. It also can be found in green leafy vegetables and peas.
- FIND A DOCTOR, A NURSE MIDWIFE OR A CLINIC you trust and make an appointment as soon as possible. Tell your clinician all medications that you are taking.
- STOP SMOKING. This addictive substance is extremely hazardous to you and your baby. Don't let others smoke around you! If you can't stop completely, cut down as much as possible.
- WEIGHT GAIN of 25 to 35 pounds during pregnancy produces the healthiest babies. Now is not the time to lose weight. A slow steady weight gain is best. If you begin gaining more than 2 pounds a week, check with your clinician or mid-wife.
- EAT A WELL-BALANCED DIET. Eat a variety of foods from each food group with a lot of fresh fruit and vegetables. Your bones and teeth will lose calcium if you don't get enough in your diet. Four cups of milk a day or 5 TUMS should do the trick. If you need help, talk to a registered dietitian. Limit your caffeine intake or do not use caffeine altogether.
- USE CONDOMS if there is any risk of HIV or other sexually transmitted infections during this pregnancy. Don't let an infection hurt your health or your baby!
- GET MODERATE EXERCISE. You should talk to your clinician about getting into an appropriate exercise regimen during pregnancy if you are not already exercising.

Good luck with your pregnancy. Take great care of yourself and your baby! Complete information about what you should do to have the healthiest baby possible is available through your clinician. Beware of using any medications and talk them over with your clinician as soon as possible. Start thinking now about nursing your baby.

Ectopic Pregnancy: The "Other" Kind

The term pregnancy usually triggers the image of a fetus developing in a woman's uterus. Most people, however, are not aware of another kind of pregnancy— ectopic—which accounts for an estimated 1 in 80 pregnancies in the United States. If an ecotpic pregnancy goes undetected, it is possible for a woman to die.

A ectopic pregnancy is when the embryo implants outside of the uterus, usually in the fallopian tubes. Women who have had pelvic inflammatory disease (PID) are at higher risk of ectopic pregnancy because of the scar tissue that results from PID. All women, however, are at some risk of ectopic pregnancy. Sudden, intense pain or cramping in the lower abdomen (usually on one side or the other), abnormal bleeding or spotting with abdominal pain when your period is late or after an abnormally light period, and fainting or dizziness lasting for more than a few seconds are all danger signs of a possible ectopic pregnancy.

If you are sexually active and experience any of these symptoms, see a health care provider immediately. A surgical technique is used to remove the embryo. The sooner an ectopic pregnancy is detected, the better the chances you have of avoiding a life-threatening emergency and the greater chance of saving your fallopian tubes.

Adoption

Making an adoption plan can be a difficult decision. It is a decision that involves courage and love. It is also a permanent choice and it takes a lot of work. There are counselors who are trained to help you weigh all of your options, decide if adoption is right for you, and help you through the process of adoption.

There are two types of adoptions: confidential and open.

<u>Confidential:</u> The birth parents and the adoptive parents will never know each other. Adoptive parents will be given background information about you and the biological father that they will need to take care of the child (e.g., medical information).

<u>Open:</u> The birth parents and the adoptive parents know something about each other. There are different levels of openness. In the least open adoption, you will be able to read about several possible adoptive families and pick the one that sounds the best for you and your baby. You will not know the family's name and they will not know your's. In a more open adoption, you and the possible adoptive family will have the opportunity to speak on the telephone and exchange first names. In an even more open adoption, you can meet the possible adoptive family at a meeting arranged by the adoption agency or an attorney. Finally, in the most open adoption, you and the adoptive parents will have the opportunity to share your full names and contact information. You can stay in contact with the family and your child by visiting, calling, or writing each other.

It is important to talk to your counselor about the type of adoption that is best for you. To get more information on adoption, or any others, contact the National Adoption Information Clearinghouse (NAIC) at naic.acf.hhs.gov (888-251-0075). You may also visit the website for the AdoptioNetwork: www.adoption.org.

Abortion
Abortion: Surgical

Abortion is the termination or ending of a pregnancy after implantation. Most surgical abortions (97%) are done by placing an instrument the size of a straw into the uterine cavity (the inside of the womb) and applying suction. This procedure is called vacuum aspiration. Each year in the United States just less than half of all pregnancies, approximately 3.5 million pregnancies, are unintended and there are about 1.5 million abortions. Anesthesia is given and is usually local (numbing the area) rather than general (being put to sleep). Usually the uterine cavity is explored with a special instrument to confirm that the abortion is complete. You will be asked to remain in the office for a brief period of time before going home.

Surgical abortion is more than 99% effective for pregnancies in the uterus. The cost of a surgical abortion depends on how far along the pregnancy is. Before 12 weeks, an abortion can cost between $130-$300 in a public clinic and is usually more expensive in a private clinic. Between 12-26 weeks, an abortion is much more expensive—between$1800-$2000 in a public clinic.

Risks of abortion include infection (up to 3%), incomplete abortion (0.5%-1.0%), bleeding (.03%-1.0%), blood clots in the uterus (less than 1%), failed abortion (0.1%-0.5%), and death (less than 1 per 100,000 abortions). Abortion is statistically safer than carrying a pregnancy to term. If performed in the first trimester, there is less than 1 death per 100,000 abortions compared to about 9 deaths per 100,000 births for women who carry a pregnancy to term. There is no increased risk of infertility, cervical problems, early labor, birth defects, or breast cancer after an initial first-trimester abortion.

Abortion: Medical

When methotrexate is used to induce a non-surgical abortion (also called a medical abortion) you will receive an injection of methotrexate, which blocks the hormone that helps the embryo to grow. This ends the pregnancy. Medical abortions can be performed very early in a pregnancy (from at least 7 weeks and up to 9 weeks). After the first visit, you will return to the clinic in 5-7 days for vaginal insertion of tablets or a suppository of another drug called misoprostol. Within 12 hours the misoprostol will cause uterine contractions, which expel the embryo. The pregnancy is usually expelled in 24-36 hours. You will be asked to remain in the office for a brief period of time before going home.

This procedure is safe and effective. Medical abortion is about 95% successful. The remaining 5% require traditional surgical procedures to complete the abortion Although not formally approved as a drug to induce an abortion, methotrexate is a drug that is widely available in the United States. It is legal and ethical for a clinician to use an approved drug for another purpose.

You may experience cramping, pain, bleeding, nausea, vomiting or diarrhea. Bleeding and the abortion process can last up to several weeks in some women. In rare cases, women can experience hair loss or low white blood cell count. Follow-up is necessary to ensure that the abortion has been completed.

Abortion: RU-486

RU-486 (mifepristone) is a pill which causes a medical abortion. It is sometimes called the "French abortion pill." It blocks the effect of progesterone on the lining of the uterus. It is followed by taking a prostaglandin called misoprostol in 48 hours later. Shortly thereafter 95% of women will abort.

In 2000, the FDA approved mifepristone, for use in combination with misoprostol, as an early option for nonsurgical abortion. To be marketed under the name Mifeprex, mifepristone is not yet widely available in U.S. clinics. You can call the National Abortion Federation's (NAF) toll-free hotline at 1-800-772-9100 for a list of health care providers who offer Mifeprex or go to the National Abortion Federation's website on early options at www.earlyoptions.org. You can also contact your local Planned Parenthood to find out if they are providing Mifeprex for early pregnancy termination. Many Planned Parenthood locations have begun offering Mifeprex as of January 2001. To find out if a local Planned Parenthood Clinic offers Mifeprex call 1-800-230-PLAN or visit PPFA's website at www.plannedparenthood.org.

No Regrets

When I was 18 years old I had unprotected sex and got pregnant. The guy I was with was supportive, but we both knew we were too young to have a child. After much thought and discussion, I decided to have an abortion. It was the best decision I have ever made—for both of us and our future children. Heather, 23 years old.

A Challenge to My Values

I was a virgin up until age 19 and was very proud of it. I am extremely religious and have been since age 12. I was attending a college when I met a beautiful girl. We became friends and began to date. One day we were both sure that we were responsible enough to be alone together at her place. We thought nothing would happen. Our kissing led to more and we ended up having unprotected intercourse. Because I had convinced myself nothing would happen I was completely unprepared. It was like going camping and convincing myself it's not going to rain and not bringing rain gear! And of course that is always when it rains – when you aren't prepared. She got pregnant. The question we had to face was "do we have this child or not?" Being incredibly religious, this wasn't a question for me. But, she wanted to have an abortion and I supported her in her decision because I felt it was her body and she who would have to give birth and raise the child. She had the abortion and we haven't spoken since. Because my sister has a little boy I often think about what may have been. Tim, 21 years old.

Oh No, What Do I Do Now!? Emergency Contraception Flow Chart

Condom breaks...
　Missed pill...
　　Forced to have sex...
　　　Got drunk and had sex...
　　　　Got carried away and didn't use protection...

↓

Has it been 72 hours or less since you had unprotected sex?

↓ ↓

YES: Call your clinician, go to your campus health center, or call 1-888-NOT-2-LATE to get the name a clinician who will prescribe emergency contraception.

NO: The effectiveness of emergency contraceptive pills is greatly decreased after 72 hours. You can still have an emergency IUD inserted.

↓

Go to a pharmacist to get the prescription filled for progestin-only pills (PLAN B or Ovrette) or combined pills (Preven or others such as Triphasil, Trilevlin, or Lo-Ovral).

Has it been 5-8 days or less since you had unprotected sex?*

↓ ↓

See your clinician or call 1-888-NOT-2-LATE to get the name of a clinician who will insert an emergency IUD.

You may need to consider other pregnancy options. See your clinician to have a pregnancy test done.

↓

If taking combined pills, take anti-nausea medicine (Dramamine II by prescription or Bonine over-the-counter).

↓

If you took anti-nausea medicine, wait one hour and then take first dose of emergency contraceptive pills. If you did not take anti-nausea medicine, take first dose immediately.

Use a contraceptive method until your next period. If you get your period within 21 days, start a contraceptive method of your choice—on that you will use consistently and correctly. If you don't get your period, see a clinician to have a pregnancy test.

↓

12 hours later, take next dose. →

NOTE: *The Copper T 380-A IUD may be inserted up to the time of implantation—about 5 days after ovulation—to prevent pregnancy. Thus, if you had unprotected intercourse 3 days before ovulation in that cycle, the IUD could be inserted up to 8 days after intercourse to prevent pregnancy.*

CHAPTER 7:
Sexually Transmitted Infections (STIs)

On the following pages, you will find important information about sexually transmitted infections (STIs). (NOTE: The terms "STI" and "STD" mean the same thing. The authors prefer the term "infection" to "disease"—as in sexually transmitted disease or STD—because "infection" has less negative connotations than "disease.") If you think you or your partner might be at risk of or might have an STI, go to your health center and get tested. If you do have a positive test, it's critical that you tell your partner so that he or she also can get tested and initiate treatment, if necessary. Open and honest communication is one way that STI transmission can be reduced. It's a good idea to start sexual health conversations early in the relationship. This way, both partners can know their status, get tested and treated if necessary, and start the relationship in an open and honest manner. Every person plays a role in this process and has a responsibility to themselves, current partners, and/or future partners to be honest when it comes to sexual health.

For more information about STIs, including HIV, contact these anonymous hotlines:

• *National AIDS Hotline: 1-800-342-AIDS*
• *National STD Hotline: 1-800-227-8922*
• *Herpes Hotline: 1-919-361-8488*

Glad They Kept in Touch

I used to think that AIDS was a serious problem that did not even remotely concern me. Then my partner's old girlfriend got in touch with him to let him know she had tested positive for HIV. It was scary for both of us to hear. But, I'd rather know, so I can make the right decisions and be aware. I'm truly grateful that she cared enough to let her ex-boyfriend know. Although I'm really nervous, we are going to get tested immediately. Eric, 25 years old.

WHAT YOU NEED TO KNOW ABOUT SEXUALLY TRANSMITTED INFECTIONS

Chlamydia

How do I get it?

Through contact between mucous membranes (cervix, urethra) and the infected persons fluids (semen and vaginal fluids). Transmission is most common with exposure through vaginal or anal sex. Research shows that casual contact (holding hands, using public restrooms, sharing food, hugging, etc.) does not transmit chlamydia.

What do I look for?

Most people with chlamydia have NO symptoms. If symptoms are present they may have the following characteristics.

• *In women:* pain or dull aching from the cervix, a heavy feeling in the pelvic area, a sharp pain during urination or intercourse, heavier than normal flow during period, breakthrough bleeding, heavy cervical discharge.
• *In Men:* Urethral discharge and/or pain with urination.

Potential problems:

In women, serious complications can occur if the infection spreads to the fallopian tubes. If untreated, chlamydia can lead to pelvic inflammatory disease (PID), a serious infection of the fallopian tubes. This could result in tubal scaring, infertility, and risk of ectopic pregnancy.

What do I do now? A number of commonly used antibiotics will cure chlamydia. Partners should be treated at the same time.

Prevention: Correctly used latex or polyutherane condoms provide protection.

I Thought "Real" Men Didn't Use Condoms

My parents went out of town for a while and my friends and I decided to have a party. We brought prostitutes over to my place. I didn't use a condom. I didn't know much about them. I thought "real men" didn't use condoms. I was wrong. A week later my parents came home and I started to notice that I had some symptoms of some kind of disease. It felt like fire was coming out of my penis when I went to the bathroom and yellow pus-like secretions dripped from the tip of my penis. I got really scared and talked with my dad. He suspected that I might have either gonorrhea or chlamydia. He took me to the doctor and I got medicine. That night my father explained all about condoms and contraception and how to avoid pregnancy and STD's. If he knew - why hadn't he told me before! After that day I have been very careful during sex and consider myself lucky to have had that experience with no permanent harm. Sid, 22 years old.

Human Papillomavirus (HPV), also known as Genital Warts

How do I get it?

Through contact – touching (hand/genital, genital/genital, genital/mouth) an infected person's lesions can transmit the virus.

What do I look for?

There are usually no symptoms, however external lesions may itch. Lesions on the skin can either be raised or flat. Lesions on the cervix can be seen only with the use of 5% acetic acid and magnification.

Potential problems:

Precancerous lesions may appear on the cervix as a result of HIV. In college-age women, it is estimated that about 10% of cervical lesions are truly precancerous. Thus, it is very important for women to get regular pap tests to help detect the presence of precancerous cell growth early. Cervical cancer is highly preventable and treatable if it is caught early.

What do I do now?

Many forms of treatment are available and all are about equally effective. If the infection is on the cervix, it is usually treated by *CRYO* (freezing) or *LASER* (burning) them off. If the infection is external some of the most common treatments are: *Aldara, Cryo, Laser, Liquid N, TCA/BCA (tri and bichloracetic acid), Podophyllin, and Interferon.* Although the symptoms (if there are any) can be treated, there is no permanent cure for HPV.

Prevention:

Barrier methods are only partially protective. With condoms, for example, lesions may be present in areas not covered by the condom. It is also possible to transmit the virus even if no lesions are present. Only total absence of any touching of infected tissue will avoid transmission.

Herpes Simplex Virus (HSV), both types I and II – "oral" and "genital"

How do I get it?

Through contact – touching (hand/genital, genital/genital, genital/mouth or mouth/mouth) an infected person's lesions can transmit the virus. Sexual intercourse is not necessary and there do not have to be lesions present to transmit the infection. Kissing an infected person or having oral sex can transmit the virus.

What do I look for?

Single or multiple fluid-filled blisters can appear on the skin especially around the genitals or mouth. They usually rupture leaving painful, shallow ulcers. These will usually go away in about 12 days. Many people report a tingling or itching sensation in the area where they are infected a few days prior to an outbreak. This is called the "prodromal period" and is also when the virus is most likely to be transmitted.

Potential problems:

Recurrent painful outbreaks (sometimes associated with stress and fatigue), chronic pain, urethral strictures. If transmission occurs to a newborn at birth, severe neurological damage or death may occur.

What do I do now?

Topical anesthetic powder or gel can be helpful in relieving symptoms. Antiviral drugs are effective if taken very early in an outbreak or continuously in a preventative regimen. Although symptoms can be treated, there is no permanent cure for herpes.

Prevention:

Barrier methods, such as condoms or dental dams (latex squares), are only partially protective. With condoms, for example, lesions may be present in areas not covered by the condom. Only total absence of any touching infected tissue will avoid transmission.

For more information on herpes, check out these two excellent web pages:
• *www.herpes.com OR www.herpeszone.com*

Excellent Communication About Herpes

I fell in love with a girl and just prior to having intercourse with her she told me she had herpes. We did not have intercourse that night. Later, as we grew closer, I came to trust her. We decided that we would cooperate in taking precautions to prevent me from getting herpes. We use condoms every time. I have never been infected. Herpes has actually made our relationship deeper and closer because we trusted and cooperated with one another. Alan, 25 years old.

Herpes From Oral Sex

One of my good friends, a freshman at the time, got herpes. She was unaware she could get it from oral sex. Also, the guy was a virgin. Cybele, 19 years old.

Pelvic Inflammatory Disease (PID)

How do I get it?

PID is often caused by sexually transmitted infections (such as chlamydia and gonorrhea) that go untreated. These infections often spread through any contact between the mucous membranes and the infected person's body fluids (vaginal fluids or semen). Transmission is most common with exposure through oral, anal, or vaginal sex. Research shows that casual contact (holding hands, using public restrooms, sharing food, hugging, etc.) does not transmit the bacteria that cause PID.

What do I look for?

PID may be completely asymptomatic. It also may be characterized by moderate to severe lower abdominal pain, fever, chills, and possibly bowel symptoms. The symptoms may be similar to appendicitis, and other severe lower abdominal conditions.

Potential problems:

PID may progress into abscesses and damage to the fallopian tubes, resulting in infertility, ectopic pregnancy, chronic pain and, in some cases, even death.

What do I do now?

PID can be cured with one or more antibiotics. The antibiotics aslo should treat for chlamydia and gonorrhea. Partners need to be treated at the same time. If the infection is severe, a hospital stay may be required to fully treat PID.

Prevention:

Correctly used latex or polyurethane condoms provide protection. Hormonal contraceptive methods (the pill, Norplant, Depo-Provera, Norplant, etc.) help prevent recurrent attacks by suppressing ovulatory menstrual cycles.

HIV and AIDS

How do I get it?

Through the exchange of body fluids (blood, vaginal fluid, semen and breast milk) with an infected individual. Transmission is most common through oral, anal, or vaginal sex and through sharing needles. Research shows that casual contact (holding hands, using public restrooms, sharing food, hugging, etc.) does not transmit HIV.

What do I look for? There are four different stages of infection:
• *Infection and seroconversion* – Flu-like symptoms and illness for about 2 weeks.
• *Incubation period* – A symptom free period that lasts a few months to many years.
• *Early symptoms* – A few months to several years with symptoms such as, but not limited to, fevers, herpes zoster (shingles) and yeast infections.
• *AIDS* – A few months to several years of opportunistic infections such as Kaposi's sarcoma, lymphoma, cervical cancer, dementia, and other neurological symptoms.

Potential problems:

Signs and symptoms of AIDS that may lead to death. Current medications can extend and improve quality of life, but, as of now, there is not a permanent cure for HIV/AIDS.

What do I do now?

Antivirals along with specific medications for complications. A variety of agencies offer services to help those living with HIV and AIDS, including assistance with housing, legal advice, food, transportation, and psychological counseling. In addition, case managers can help get reduced-cost or free medication.

Prevention:

Correctly used condoms, either latex or polyurethane, provide protection. Avoid sharing needles, particularly for IV drug use. If needles are shared, they must be cleaned thoroughly with bleach and/or sterilized solutions before the next use.

My Partner Took Off The Condom
I waited over 18 years before deciding to have intercourse. I don't regret it, but my partner did not want me to use a condom because she said it didn't feel as good. I used one but half-way through she took it off. As much as I trusted her I have always had this horrible nagging fear in the back of my mind that I may have been infected with HIV that time with her. I am scared to get tested, but there isn't a day that goes by that I am not haunted with the thought that I am infected and that my life will end soon. Jeffrey, 18 years old.

More Information on HIV: *Because HIV/AIDS is a complex disease that has impacted the lives of many people - both infected and affected - we have included the following section with more information on HIV/AIDS.*

HIV is a virus that affects human beings by destroying the body armor, called the immune system. When the immune system becomes weakened the body can no longer defend itself against the germs and sickness that we commonly pick up in the air, from other people, on doorknobs, and so on. When a person has no ability to fight off any germs that a person is considered to have AIDS. AIDS is a compilation of many sicknesses and health complications, commonly referred to as opportunistic infections. It is linguistically and physically not really possible to die of AIDS. It would be more accurate to say that someone died due to complications from any number of possible illnesses that commonly afflict people with an impaired immune system.

There are a variety of misconceptions about how HIV is transmitted. At this moment, we know from research that HIV is NOT transmitted through urine, sweat, tears, feces, or saliva. It is also not transmitted by mosquitoes, on toilet seats, from sharing utensils or food, or through any casual contact (e.g., hugging, kissing, or shaking hands). HIV can be transmitted through blood, semen, vaginal fluids, and breast milk. Thus, any behaviors where these fluids can be exchanged—sexual behaviors, sharing IV drug needles, breastfeeding, or from mother to child during pregnancy—place an individual at risk of HIV.

People with HIV are often viewed as having something awful. In reality, a person with HIV may be more accurately described as *not* having something important— that is, an intact immune system. A person with an intact immune system will have between 1200 and 800 T-cells (cells that help fight off germs and sickness). When a person becomes infected with HIV, their T-cells are disabled so that the number of cells that protects them plummets. Eventually, the number of T-cells will reach 200. At this point, virtually anything—even a common cold—could lead to death. The medical definition of AIDS is when a person has a T-cell count of 200 and experiences any opportunistic infection.

People *lacking* education about this virus are the people that most often end up *lacking* their immune system. Hopefully, now that you know how people get infected and what does and does not not transmit HIV you can prevent yourself and your loved ones from being infected.

HIV Resources:

- National AIDS Hotline: 1-800-342-AIDS
- Critical Path AIDS Project: www.critpath.org
- National CDC Prevention Information Network: www.cdcnpin.org
- AEGIS - the largest HIV/AIDS website in the world. Updated hourly: www.aegis.com

Gonorrhea

How do I get it?

Through contact of mucous membranes (cervix, urethra) with infected person's body fluids (semen and vaginal fluids). Transmission is most common through vagi-nal or anal sex. Research shows that casual contact (holding hands, using public rest-rooms, sharing food, hugging, etc.) does not transmit gonorrhea.

What do I look for? Many of the same symptoms as chlamydia:
• *In women:* pain or dull aching from the cervix, a heavy feeling in the pelvic area, a sharp pain during urination or intercourse, heavier than normal flow during your period, breakthrough bleeding, heavy cervical discharge.
• *In Men:* Urethral discharge and/or pain with urination.

Potential problems:

In many women, serious complications can occur if the infection goes untreated and reaches the fallopian tubes. Such complications may result in pelvic inflamma-tory disease (PID), which may lead to tubal scarring, infertility, and risk of ectopic pregnancy.

What do I do now?

A number of commonly used antibiotics will cure gonorrhea. Partners must be treated at the same time.

Prevention: Correctly used condoms, either latex or polyurethane, provide protection.

Hepatitis B

How do I get it?

Through contact of mucous membranes (cervix, urethra) with infected person's body fluid (semen, saliva, blood and mucus). Transmission is most common with exposure through vaginal or anal sex. Research shows that casual contact (holding hands, using public restrooms, sharing food, hugging, etc.) does not transmit hepatitis B.

What do I look for?

At first, usually asymptomatic (no symptoms). If the infection progresses, symptoms such as high fever, fatigue, jaundice (yellowish skin), diarrhea, nausea and vomiting, and abdominal pain can occur.

Potential problems: Cirrhosis, liver cancer, liver failure, and death.

What do I do now?

Although symptoms can be treated, there is no cure for hepatitis and the infection has to run its course. However, there are vaccines available which are very effective. Recently, it has been recommended that all infants and adolescents be immunized, as well as those at risk. Many colleges and universities require students to be vaccinated before enrollment.

Prevention: Vaccination.

Syphilis

How do I get it?
Through the exchange of fluids and contact. Through contact of mucous membranes (cervix, urethra) with infected person's body fluid (semen, saliva, blood and vaginal fluids). Transmission is most common through vaginal or anal sex. Syphilis can also be transmitted through contact – touching the area of infection (hand/genital, genital/genital, genital/mouth) can transmit cells containing the infection.

What do I look for? Occurs in three stages: primary, secondary, and latent.
• *Primary:* Painless ulcer (chancre).
• *Secondary:* Could have a rash generally on the palms of the hands and bottoms of the feet, lymph node enlargement, and spotty baldness, among other symptoms.
• *Latent:* No clinical signs, but vascular and neurological damage may occur.

Potential problems:
If left untreated, may result in brain damage, insanity, and, in some cases, death.

What do I do now?
Syphilis is curable if treated. However, any damage that has already occurred is irreversible. The most common medication given to somebody with syphilis is penicillin.

Prevention: Correctly used latex or polyurethane condoms provide protection.

CHAPTER 8:
Sexual Harassment and Assault

Sexual Harassment

In the past decade, sexual harassment has come to the forefront of academic, workplace, and political discussions, allowing many people to speak out and seek help in stopping harassment. On the flip side, because the definition of harassment is often gray and varies from institution to institution, it is still difficult in some cases to label certain actions or situations harassment. According to the U.S. Equal Employment Opportunity Commission, sexual harassment involves "unwelcome sexual advances, requests for sexual favors, and other verbal or physical conduct of a sexual nature constitutes sexual harassment when submission to or rejection of this conduct explicitly or implicitly affects an individual's employment, unreasonably interferes with an individual's work performance or creates an intimidating, hostile or offensive work environment."

Sexual harassment can occur in a variety of circumstances, including but not limited to the following:

• *The person subjected to sexual harassment as well as the harasser may be female or male. Sexual harassment can occur between members of the same gender.*
• *The harasser can be a professor, supervisor, an agent of the employer, a supervisor in another area, a peer, or person unrelated to the college or university.*
• *Harassment can affect people beyond the person directly harassed to include anyone affected by the offensive conduct.*
• *The harasser's conduct must be unwelcome and unwanted.*

It is helpful for the person who has been harassed to directly inform the harasser that the conduct is unwelcome and must stop. The person should notify appropriate university officials to report the harassment.

Sexual Assault, Sexual Abuse, and Rape

*According to Campus Outreach Services, women aged 15-24 run a greater risk of being raped than any other population group. More specifically, a woman is most likely to experience an assault during her **first two months of college**. The highest percentages of rape occur in areas where there is the **greatest inequality between genders**, including fraternity houses, the military and football-related events.*

The legal definitions of these terms vary from state to state and college to college. For instance, in some states, rape is defined only as forced intercourse on a female by a male, while in others both a male and a female can be considered legally a victim or perpetrator of rape.

Regardless of legal definitions, any person—male, female, transgendered, gay, lesbian, bi, straight, married, single, partnered, young, old, rich, poor, and so on—can be sexually assaulted, abused, or raped. Nevertheless, our society often defines rape with a female as the victim and a male as the assailant. This definition does reflect statistics. According to the National Victim Center and the Crime Victims Research and Treatment Center, women in the U.S. have a 1 in 5 lifetime risk of being raped and a 1 in 3 chance if they are in college. Many of these survivors suffer in silence and never feel comfortable enough to tell those people closest to them. Approximately 68% of rape survivors knew their assailant and approximately 28% of survivors are raped by husbands or boyfriends, 35% by acquaintances, and 5% by other relatives.

It is incorrect, however, to assume that men cannot be raped and assaulted as well or that rape is only a heterosexual crime. A survey conducted for the United States Bureau of Justice Statistics found that the rapes of males reported to their interviewers were 26% of the number of completed rapes reported by females in the same survey; when applied to the national population that would be about 12,300 rapes of males per year. However, these figures are believed to be underestimates due to a reluctance of male survivors to identify themselves in interviews. Rape of a woman by another woman also can occur, although it is rarely reported.

Whether an attacker uses brutal force, alcohol or other drugs, emotional coercion, or verbal threats, or if the person fights, screams, or silently submits, sexual violence is a crime. Sexual assault, abuse, and rape are not about sex. Rather, these are acts of violence and aggression fueled by a desire for power, control, and dominance over another person. The fact that they involve sexual acts and sexual body parts makes them particularly sensitive, secretive, and potentially more traumatizing and violating than other crimes.

It is just as important to point out that a person is not raped because of revealing clothes, flirtatious behavior, sexual history, religion, or race and ethnicity. No one "deserves" to be raped and no one ever "asks" for rape. Sexual assault and sexual abuse are crimes committed by the attacker and not the attacked.

The distinction between sexual assault and abuse generally have to do with the type of contact. Sexual assault is often defined as "sexual intercourse or sexual intrusion" while sexual abuse is defined more broadly as "sexual contact." Sexual abuse does not always include physical violence. For example, obscene phone calls can be considered abusive. In the end, it is important to familiarize yourself with your college or university policies on sexual assault, abuse, and rape because definitions can vary greatly. A general guideline, however, is this: **Any sexual contact that is unwanted, coercive, or forced is WRONG and can be considered assault, abuse, and/or rape.**

The long-term effects of sexual assault and abuse (whether it is rape, incest, sexual violence, harassment, coercion, molestation, or any other kind of unwanted contact) can be physically, emotionally, and psychologically detrimental. Counseling can help survivors come to terms with what happened to them in a safe environment and move forward with their lives and relationships.

This chapter attempts to be accessible to anyone, since everyone is at risk of rape, assault, and abuse. Nevertheless, because women are most often the survivors of rape and sexual assault, it is necessary to pay extra attention to women's issues. Women on college campuses need to be especially aware. For more information about or help in coping with rape, sexual assault, and sexual abuse:

- Rape, Abuse, and Incest National Network (RAINN): 1-800-636-HOPE
- National Resource Center on Violence: 1-800-537-2238
- Centers for Disease Control Rape Hotline: 1-800-344-7432 Spanish
  1-800-243-7889 Hearing Imapired
  1-800-342-2437 English

Childhood Trauma

I was raped at the age of six by an eighteen year-old babysitter. I know only the physical and emotional pain of sex from this experience. It has made me celibate for a long time. Most people consider me a "virgin," but I must be the only "virgin" with vivid nightmares of being raped. Through therapy, I am able to work through a lot of the pain and anger I have been carrying around throughout life. It does get easier, but the memory will always be there. Renee, 18 years old.

Something Changed
Upon seeing a girl for the second time after getting quite physical the first time, we began to again. In the middle of foreplay she got really quiet and hesitant. Before I knew what I was doing, I felt like I was forcing myself on her. We stopped and talked it out. That instance changed my views on sex, giving me a greater respect. Chen, 21 years old.

Loving Partner Provides Support After Abuse
I repressed this memory for years. I still don't remember exactly what happened. I remember that my mother would leave me with my uncle when I needed a babysitter. He molested me. I don't remember the specifics, but I know he asked me "is that what you like?" and told me that there was no reason to feel bad and that I could never tell anyone. Since then I have had real troubles with intimacy and relationships. I have been going out with a wonderful woman for two years and I am getting better at trusting people. During my first two years of college I was so depressed and ashamed of what happened to me I would get drunk every weekend and pass out. I must have had 40 sex partners. But now, with the help of my current girlfriend, things are slowly getting better. Michael, 23 years old.

From Now On, I'll Follow My Instincts
Two summers ago I went to my high school to walk around the track. Only two other people were walking around, and after half a lap or so I noticed that they had left. It was then that I noticed a man walking near the bleachers. I was scared and concerned but I didn't want him to think I thought he was suspicious so I kept walking. As I got around to the side where he was he jumped out, with his pants around his ankles, and started masturbating. I ran past him and went and called the police. Needless to say, I followed my gut instincts from then on and didn't let my fear of offending anyone put me in danger! It could have been much worse. Terina, 19 years old.

Pressured Into Unwanted Sex
Something unexpected happened to me. I was pressured to have sex and I gave in. I wasn't sure if I wanted it or not. It was over so fast I couldn't say no. He kept telling me that I was a tease and that I was so hot. He said I needed sex and he was the guy to give it to me. I was afraid of what would happen if I didn't. I was a little afraid of him and yet I liked the flattery, even though he was crude. The experience has left me feeling guilty and ashamed that I was unable to make a decision and that I just let it happen. Mary, 22 years old.

What To Do If You Have Been Sexually Assaulted

Do not bathe, wash, or dispose of your clothes yet.
Your body and clothes can provide important evidence
for catching and prosecuting the person who sexually
assaulted you.

Tell someone you trust what happened to you—a friend,
partner, parent or other relative, doctor, counselor, or a
hotline. The number for the National Rape Crisis
Hotline is 1-800-656-HOPE.

Go to a hospital or clinic as soon as possible. Even if
you do not want to press charges, you may have been
injured, acquired a sexually transmitted infection, or may
become pregnancy (and therefore may want to consider
emergency contraception).

Know that the decision to press charges will be your
decision—it is up to you to do what you feel is best for
your situation.

In the month following the assault, get tested for sexually
transmitted infections, HIV, and pregnancy.

Consider seeking help from a counselor or therapist—you
may have any number of emotions such as fear, confusion,
denial, anger, helplessness, guilt, depression, or self-blame.
It can help to process these feelings with someone who is
trained to counsel sexual assault survivors.

Remember, you did not deserve this and are not to
blame. Sexual assault is a violent crime. No one
deserves to have be sexually assaulted, raped, or abused.

What To Do If You Are the Friend of a Survivor of Sexual Assault

If you have a friend that is a survivor of sexual assault there are a variety of things you can do to be helpful and supportive:

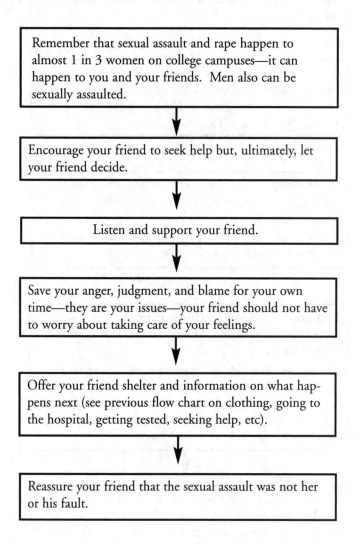

Remember that sexual assault and rape happen to almost 1 in 3 women on college campuses—it can happen to you and your friends. Men also can be sexually assaulted.

Encourage your friend to seek help but, ultimately, let your friend decide.

Listen and support your friend.

Save your anger, judgment, and blame for your own time—they are your issues—your friend should not have to worry about taking care of your feelings.

Offer your friend shelter and information on what happens next (see previous flow chart on clothing, going to the hospital, getting tested, seeking help, etc).

Reassure your friend that the sexual assault was not her or his fault.

Clear Communication Can Help Prevent Misunderstanding: The Antioch Policy

According to a Washington, D.C. Rape Crisis Clinic, 1 out of every 3 women will be the victim of sexual assault during her lifetime. Statistics like these prompted students at Ohio's Antioch College to write and implement policies aimed at preventing sexual assault and abuse. The policy can be summed up with the idea that it is necessary to obtain a clear affirmative response before proceeding with any and all sexual intimacy.

In 1993, the student body organized, proposed, and instituted a Sexual Violence and Safety Policy, sometimes referred to as the "Antioch Policy," which focuses on the specifics of sexual offense. All students are responsible for knowing the elements of the policy. While Antioch is a small college, the policy guidelines are applicable for all colleges, universities, and on a broader range, all people.

Some of the Antioch guidelines you can adopt are:
• All sexual contact and conduct between any two people must be consensual.
• Consent must be obtained verbally before there is any sexual contact or conduct.
• For truly consensual sex, you and your partner(s) should be sober.
• To knowingly take advantage of someone who is under the influence of alcohol, drugs, and/or prescribed medication is not acceptable.
• If the level of sexual intimacy increases during interaction (i.e., if two people move from kissing while fully clothed to undressing for direct physical contact), the people involved need to express their clear verbal consent before moving to the next level.
• If one person wants to initiate moving to a higher level of sexual intimacy during an interaction, that person is responsible for getting the verbal consent of the other person involved before moving to the next level.
• If you have had a particular level of sexual intimacy before with someone, you must still ask each and every time.
• If you have a sexually transmitted infection, you must disclose it to a potential sexual partner before sexual contact is made.
• Never make assumptions about consent.
• Silence does not mean consent.

The Antioch policy received much controversial media attention after its inception. Critics argued that the college took political correctness to an extreme while supporters complimented the college for initiating a social norm that emphasizes responsibility, respect, and explicit disapproval of sexual assault and abuse. Despite the controversy, the intent of the Antioch policy is clear—open communication and respect are the keys to consensual sexual activity. The authors believe that applying these guidelines to your sexual relationships in college can be an important part of preventing misunderstanding, date rape, and sexual assault.

CHAPTER 9:
Closure

Our collaborative vision is to help people learn how to implement and practice the Sexual Etiquette Guidelines. We hope our book has helped you, the reader, celebrate yourself in ways that brings great joy to your life while not harming others or interfering with others' rights to pursue happiness. If you are having trouble finding pleasure in life, need information, or someone to listen, or are harming others, we hope that our resources provide you with the support necessary. We deeply believe that every person who reads this book will be better prepared to live in ways that exemplify the humanitarian values and principles outlined in the Guidelines. An educator named Kurt Hahn once wrote, *"There is more in us than we know. If we can be made to see it, perhaps for the rest of our lives we will be unwilling to settle for less."* We hope our book has illuminated the truly wonderful potential that is contained within each of you—about sexuality and beyond—and encouraged each of you never to settle for less.

Our aim is to reduce some of the silence, shame, guilt, embarrassment, and confusion around sexuality. If you believe that the ideas contained in this book are worthwhile, we encourage you to support sexuality education and your right to accurate and reliable information regarding health, reproduction, and relationships. Hopefully, this book has helped you and will continue to help prevent the potentially negative consequences of sexuality while embracing the potentially beautiful and pleasurable aspects of sexuality!

There is still a lot of work to be done regarding how we manage and conduct human relationships. Watch the news on any given night, it will be clear that our culture is in desperate need of relational help. Healthy relationships do not just happen. They take commitment, work, and study. These sentiments were best expressed by Madeline Albright when she spoke at the University of California. "During the century just passed," she said, "we humans learned how to transplant hearts, fly spaceships, clone sheep, and squeeze a library's worth of data into a single slender disc. But as the world events reflect, we remain far from mastering the art of human relations. We have invented no technology that will guide us to the destinations that matter most. After two world wars, the Holocaust, multiple genocides, we must ask how long it will be before we are able to rise above the national, racial, and gender distinctions that divide us, and embrace the common humanity that binds us." This quote embodies our message to you.

We challenge you to work towards maintaining and nurturing healthy and loving relationships. There has never been, and there never will be, anything as important as close, caring, honest, supportive, and loving relationships. Remember, live life just for today because today is a gift—that's why they call it the present.

—*Bob, Shannon, Erika & Chris*

CHAPTER 10:
Where To Get More Information

Believe it or not, this book just scratches the surface about all there is to know and learn about sexuality! We know that each of you has individual needs and hope that you will find what you need in *Sexual Etiquette 101* to point you in the right direction toward sexual health and fulfillment. Fortunately, resources on various aspects of sexuality continue to increase. Listed below are national hotlines and telephone numbers, websites, and contact information for several prominent sexuality organizations. All the resources listed throughout the book are compiled here as well as additional resources that are not listed elsewhere in the book. Along with using these resources for yourself, please share this list with friends and family who are in need of information, help, or support.

NATIONAL HOTLINES AND TELEPHONE NUMBERS

National Suicide Hotline	1-800-SUICIDE
Emergency Contraception Hotline	1-888-Not-2-Late
National Runaway Switchboard	1-800-621-4000
CDC National AIDS Hotline	1-800-342-AIDS
Gay Men's Health Crisis Hotline	1-800-AIDS-NYC
National STD Hotline	1-800-227-8922
National Herpes Hotline	1-919-361-8488
National Gay and Lesbian Hotline	1-888-843-4564
National Child Abuse Hotline	1-800-422-4453
Domestic Violence Hotline	1-800-942-6906
Rape, Abuse, and Incest National Network (RAINN)	1-800-656-HOPE
National Resource Center on Violence	1-800-537-2238
Centers for Disease Control Rape Hotline	1-800-344-7432 Spanish
	1-800-243-7889 Hearing Imapired
	1-800-342-2437 English
Drug Abuse Hotline	1-800-821-4357
Narcotics Anonymous	1-818-773-9999

12 Step Self-Help Program Hotline	1-800-905-8666
National Pregnancy Hotline	1-800-311-2229
National Abortion Federation	1-800-772-9100
National Adoption Clearinghouse	1-888-251-0075
National Depressive and Manic- Depressive Association	1-800-826-3632
Depression: Awareness, Recognition & Treatment (DART)	1-800-421-4211
Eating Disorders and Prevention, Inc.	1-800-931-2237
Planned Parenthood	1-800-230-PLAN

WEBSITES

HIV/AIDS/STDs

AIDS Education Global Information System	www.aegis.com
HIV/AIDS Youth Informational Website	www.youthhiv.org
AIDS Education Training Centers	www.AIDS-ed.org
Critical Path AIDS Project	www.critpath.org
National Centers for Disease Control Prevention Information Network	www.cdcnpin.org
Centers for Disease Control National Health Statistics	www.cdc.gov/nchs
American Social Health Association	www.ashastd.org
Herpes Information Resource	www.herpes.com
The Herpes Help	www.Herpeshelp.com

Contraception/Family Planning

Managing Contraception	www.managingcontraception.com
Birth Control Information and Products	www.birthcontrol.com
Emergency Contraception	www.opr.princeton.edu
	www.go2planB.com
	www.PREVEN.com
Adoption Network	www.adoption.org

National Abortion Center	www.nac.adopt.org
National Abortion Rights Action League	www.naral.org
National Abortion Federation	www.prochoice.org

Sexuality (General)

Alan Guttmacher Institute	www.agi-usa.org
Advocates for Youth	www.advocatesforyouth.org
Sexuality Information and Education Council for the United States	www.siecus.org
Planned Parenthood Federation of America	www.plannedparenthood.org
Human Sexuality, Inc.	www.howtohavegoodsex.com
Sexual Health Network	www.sexualhealth.com
Coalition for Positive Sexuality	www.positive.org
Go Ask Alice! Columbia University's Health Education Program	www.goaskalice.columbia.edu
National Campaign to Prevent Teen Pregnancy	www.teenpregnancy.org
Spanish Sexuality Website	www.gentejoven.org.mx

Gay, Lesbian, Bisexual, Transgendered (GLBT)

Human Rights Campaign	www.hrc.org
National Coming Out Project	www.hrc.org/ncop/index.html
Parents, Families, and Friends of Lesbians and Gays (PFLAG)	www.pflag.org
!Outproud!	www.outproud.com
Gay Men's Health Crisis	www.gmhc.org
National Gay and Lesbian Task Force	www.ngltf.org
Transgender Forum and Resource Center	www.tgforum.com
Intersex Society of North America	www.isna.org
Youth Resource (a project of Advocates for Youth)	www.youthresource.com

International Foundation for Gender Education	www.ifge.org
Renaissance Transgender Association	www.ren.org
GLBT Youth Information Website	www.youth.org
Spanish GLBT Informational Website	www.ambientejoven.org

Rape, Sexual Abuse, Assault, and Harassment

| Safer Society Foundation, Inc. | www.safersociety.org |

Mental Health/Depression/Eating Disorders

National Depressive and Manic-Depressive Association	www.ndmda.org
Recovery, Inc.	www.recovery-inc.com
Eating Disorders and Prevention, Inc.	www.edap.org
Anorexia Nervosa and Related Eating Disorders, Inc.	www.anred.com
Support, Concern, and Resources for Eating Disorders (S.C.a.R.E.D.)	www.eating-disorder.org

Breast/Testicular Cancer

American Cancer Society	www.cancer.org
The Testicular Cancer Resource Center	www.acor.org/diseases/TC
Lance Armstrong Foundation	www.laf.org
American Cancer Society Breast Cancer Network	www.cancer.org/bcn/index.html
Susan G. Komen Breast Cancer Foundation	www.komen.org

Disability and Sexuality

| Sexual Health Network | www.sexualhealth.com |
| Disability Cool | www.geocities.com/HotSprings/7319/discool.htm |

SEXUALITY ORGANIZATIONS

SEXUALITY ORGANIZATIONS

American Academy of Clinical Sexologists,
American Board of Sexology
1929 18th Street NW, Suite 1166
Washington, DC 20009

American Association of Sex Educators, Counselors and Therapists (AASECT)
P.O. Box 5488
Richmond, VA 23220-0488
Phone: 804-644-3288
Fax: 804-644-3290
www.aasect.org

International Academy of Sex Research (IASR)
Child and Family Studies Center
Clarke Institute of Psychology
250 College Street
Toronto, Ontario M5T 1R8
Canada

The Kinsey Institute for Sex, Gender and Reproduction
313 Morrison Hall
Indiana University
Bloomington, IN 47405
www.indiana.edu/~kinsey/

Sexuality Information and Education Council of the United States (SIECUS)
130 West 42nd Street,
Suite 350
New York, NY 10036-7802
Phone: 212-819-9770
Fax: 212-819-9776
www.siecus.org

The Society for the Scientific Study of Sex (SSSS)
P.O. Box 416
Allentown, PA 18105
610-530-2483
www.sexscience.org

World Association of Sexology
C/o Eli Coleman, Secretary General and Treasurer
University of Minnesota Medical School
1300 South Second Street, Suite 180
Minneapolis, MN 55454

New 18th Revised Edition
900 Pages of New and Vital Information

6"x9" Actual Size

We have drawn on experts throughout the country to author chapters of this **NEW book**. For the first time, color photos of all pills will appear in the new edition of **Contraceptive Technology 18th**.

Included will be the new WHO medical eligibility criteria for starting contraceptive methods, the updated failure rates from James Trussell and CDC's most recent STD treatments and guidelines.

- The Patch, The Ring and the LNG Intrauterine System
- Menopause Management Today
- All new reproductive cancer screening recommendations
- Extensive listing of 800 numbers and websites for Family Planning related topics
- Medical abortion
- Office based infertility workups

Also, look for the new color section of all the oral contraceptive pills, which makes communicating with patients so much easier.

Order online: www.ManagingContraception.com

5/2004

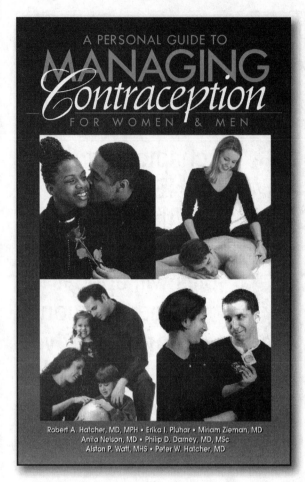

Para las Mujeres y los Hombres todo Sexual Activos

NEW

una guía para
la salud reproductiva
y la anticoncepción

{ la planificación familiar }

Robert A. Hatcher, MD, MPH

Erika I. Pluhar, PhD

Miriam Zieman, MD

Anita Nelson, MD

Philip Darney, MD, MSc

Peter W. Hatcher, MD

Traducción al español:

Carlos Moisa, MD

Myriam Hernández-Jennings, MA

Claudia Burnham, BS

Jay Miranda, BA

The Spanish Version of *A Personal Guide to Managing Contraception*

Devices & Desires
A History of Contraceptives in America

A BEST SELLER

"Andrea Tone's fascinating book, Devices and Desires, takes the wraps off birth control's long journey from illegality in the nineteenth century to legality in the twentieth. Women today are still suffering the aftereffects, not only from their less than perfect methods of birth control, but also from America's failure to develop better methods for all women at all times during their reproductive lives. How couples 'made do' with the often faulty methods available makes one marvel at our human ingenuity. Devices and Desires is must reading for anyone interested in women's rights and health."

Alexander Sanger
Chair
International Planned Parenthood Council

Brothel: Mustang Ranch and Its Women

A Fun Read and Educational

A brave young doctor's intimate and unforgettable account of the lives of the women who work in America's largest brothel.

"This well-written, nonjudgmental, informative book helps to replace ignorance with understanding concerning the lives and attitudes of women involved in legal prostitution, as well as their customers. It could serve as a light at the end of a very long tunnel, and form the basis of both moral and legal discussions about prostitution in the future."

Jocelyn Elders, MD

Available in Paperback only.

Alexa Albert is a graduate of Brown University and Harvard Medical School. She has written and lectured widely on issues of public health and prostitution and was named one of **Mirabella's 1,000 Women for the Nineties** for her work with Nevada's legal prostitutes. She currently lives with her husband and daughter in Seattle, where she is completing her residency.

Order online: www.ManagingContraception.com

Big Question!
With all the talk about continuous use of pills...

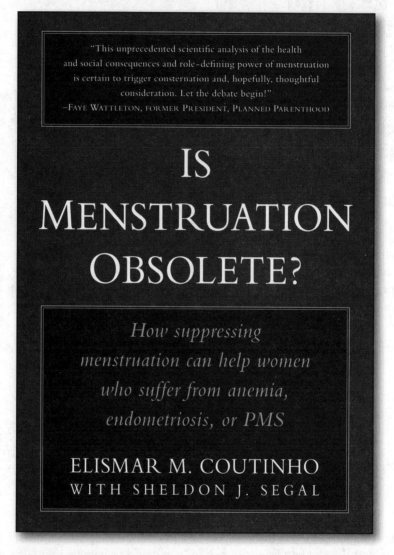

"This unprecedented scientific analysis of the health and social consequences and role-defining power of menstruation is certain to trigger consternation and, hopefully, thoughtful consideration. Let the debate begin!"
—FAYE WATTLETON, FORMER PRESIDENT, PLANNED PARENTHOOD

IS MENSTRUATION OBSOLETE?

How suppressing menstruation can help women who suffer from anemia, endometriosis, or PMS

ELISMAR M. COUTINHO

WITH SHELDON J. SEGAL

Is Menstruation Obsolete? argues that regular monthly bleeding is not the natural state of women and that it actually places them at risk of several medical conditions of varying severity. The authors maintain that while menstruation may be culturally significant, it is not medically meaningful. Moreover, they propose that suppressing menstruation has remarkable health advantages.

For College Students & All Young Adults (18-22)

More than 250,000 distributed to colleges and universities throughout the U.S.

Sexual Etiquette 101 and More

This book contains stories, resources, ideas, and other valuable tools to help you successfully navigate the often confusing world of relationships and sexuality. Through this book, we aim to provide you with information to help you prevent the possibly negative and harmful side of sexuality so that you can enjoy the pleasurable and beautiful side of sexuality and make decisions that are right for you.

- Outercourse (what it is and why you may love it)
- Selecting a method of contraception that will work for you
- Why condoms are so important
- What to do if you are sexually assaulted
- Making sexual behavior mutual & consensual
- What it takes for abstinence to work
- Contemporary HIV/AIDS issues
- Breaking-up
- Communication tips throughout

"With all the controversy in this country today about the specifics of sex education, there is one indisputable fact: sex education is necessary in order to overcome not just sexual problems suffered by Americans of all ages, but to ensure healthier kids, improve people's quality of life, and help everyone establish loving relationships… Sexual Etiquette 101 does this! "

Judy Kuriansky, Ph.D.
Adjunct Professor of Psychology,
Columbia Univ. Teachers College
Author, The Complete Idiot's Guide to Dating

160 pages - 6x9

Order online: www.ManagingContraception.com

For Adolescents Age 13-18

The Quest for Excellence is a must for teaching and learning reproductive health. Deals with **"How to Say No"** and building self-esteem around a healthy sexual identity. **For teenagers and parents of teenagers.**

- Moving through Adolescence into Adulthood
- Developing Self-Esteem
- Coping with Stress
- Human Sexuality
- 10 Rules to Sexual Etiquette
- Choosing a Contraceptive
- Keeping Yourself Healthy
- Alcohol & Drug Issues
- Sexual Abuse, Sexual Assault & Rape

182 pages - 3.5x5.5

"I found The Quest for Excellence to be a great resource for our youth program entitled 'Sexuality as a Gift from God.' It approaches sexual issues holistically, as a part of the many issues youth encounter on a daily basis. I will recommend it to both parents and youth as they deal with the complex changes and issues of adolescence."
The Rev. Brian C. Sullivan

Emergency Contraceptive Kits

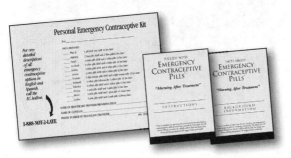

The kit contains:
- Complete instructions including the critical time frame
- Success with Emergency Contraceptive Pills
- Condoms (so you won't need Emergency Contraceptive Pills)
- 99 ways to have fun sexually without getting pregnant or STIs (so you won't need Emergency Contraceptive Pills)
- **All the clinician does is add the pills!**

Order online: www.ManagingContraception.com

Something Nice To Do 365 Days A Year

Something Nice to Do 365 Days a Year is more than a calendar. It is stories of people doing nice things for others or for themselves. Saying thank you repeatedly, leaving "I love you" notes, picking flowers and bringing them to a friend who is sick, starting the day with a tough task on your list and listening actively. People who have used this book, love it! Try it and you'll agree.

Bob Hatcher

Blind Trust: A Child's Legacy

This is a story of hope and healing. It is about coming of age in the deep South, about falling down and getting up again, about learning to cope, and about finding life worth living, after all.

"What happened to Karen Austin should never happen to any child. But she survived, and her insights will bring tears to your eyes. You will be furious as this personal memoir pulls you inside an abused child's world to understand her confusion as well as the pervasive and long lasting consequences of child abuse."

Robert A. Hatcher, MD, MPH
Professor of Gynecology and Obstetrics
Emory University School of Medicine

Order Form

	Cost		Quantity	Total
Contraceptive Technology - 18th Edition				
For your desk	1-24	59.95 ea		
	25-50	49.95 ea		
	51-500	39.95 ea		
A Pocket Guide to Managing Contraception 2004-2005 (for clinicians)				
For your pocket	1-99	10.00 ea		
	100-199	9.00 ea		
	200-299	8.00 ea		
	300	6.00 ea		
La Planificación Familiar (for Spanish speaking public)				
Managing Contraception for Women and Men	1-99	16.95 ea		
	100-199	12.95 ea		
Personal Guide to Managing Contraception for Women and Men (for the general public)				
	1-99	14.95 ea		
	100-199	11.95 ea		
Something Nice Calendar				
	1-9	15.00 ea		
	10-499	12.00 ea		
Sexual Etiquette 101 & More (College Students)				
	1-24	5.95 ea		
	25-499	2.50 ea		
	500-999	2.00 ea		
Quest for Excellence (For Adolescents)				
	1-24	5.95 ea		
	25-499	2.50 ea		
	500-999	2.00 ea		
Emergency Contraceptive Kits				
	10 (minimum)	35.00		
	11-100	3.00 ea		
	101-500	2.50 ea		
Blind Trust: A Child's Legacy		13.95 ea		
Devices & Desires - A History of Contraceptives in America				
Brothel: Mustang Ranch and Its Women		30.00 ea		
		14.95 ea		
Is Menstruation Obsolete?				
		24.00 ea		

CALL FOR PRICES ON LARGER QUANTITIES

Prices subject to change without notice.   **Sub total**

continue on next page

BRIDGING THE GAP
COMMUNICATIONS, INC.

Sub total _____

Georgia locations add 7% sales tax _____

15% Shipping • (CALL FOR INTERNATIONAL SHIPPING) _____

Add $1 Handling Fee _____

Total Enclosed _____

SHIP TO: Name: _____

Organization: _____

Address: _____

_____ Zip _____

Phone No. _____ Fax No. _____

Email _____

We accept check or credit cards: VISA, MasterCard, Discover & American Express, Purchase

Credit Card No. _____ Expiration Date: _____

Signature: _____ (Required)

P.O. # (Organizations Only) _____

Make checks payable to Bridging the Gap Communications. Payment required with all orders. Organization may use purchase orders.

Mail or Fax this ORDER FORM with your payment to:
Bridging the Gap Communications
P.O. Box 888 • Dawsonville, GA 30534

Phone: (706) 265-7435 • Fax: (706) 265-6009
www.ManagingContraception.com
email: info@managingcontraception.com

The **mission** of Bridging The Gap Foundation is to improve reproductive health and contraceptive decision-making of women and men by providing up-to-date educational resources to the physicians, nurses and public health leaders of tomorrow.

Our **vision** is to provide educational resources to the health care providers of tomorrow to help ensure informed choices, better service, access, happier and more successful contraceptors, competent clinicians, fewer unintended pregnancies and disease prevention.

CONTEMPORARY FORUMS

11900 Silvergate Drive
Dublin, CA 94568-2213
Phone: (800) 377-7707
Online: www.contemporaryforums.com

For the most up-to-date information delivered in a personable manner from the most authoritative sources, attend a Contraceptive Technology Conference.

For dates and locations, call Contemporary Forums at 800-329-9923 or access online at www.contemporaryforums.com

05/2004

A Pocket Guide to Managing Contraception
2004-2005 Edition

- Menstrual Cycle
- Screening & Risk Assessment by Age
- Counseling, Sexual HX/ Dysfunction, Adolescent Issues
- Perimenopause, Menopause, HRT
- Pregnancy Preplanning/Tests, PP, Termination
- Timing Issues, Choosing a Method, Failure Rates
- Abstinence, Breast-Feeding, FAM
- Condoms for Men and Women
- Barriers: Cap, Diaphragm, Spermicides, Withdrawal
- Emergency Contraception: COCS, POPS, IUD, RU-486
- Intrauterine Contraceptives
- Combined Contraceptives: Pills, Patches, Injections, Rings
- Progestin-Only Contraceptives: Pills, Injections, Implants
- Sterilization & Future Methods
- CDC STI Treatments
- WHO Medical Eligibility Criteria & Color Photos of Pills

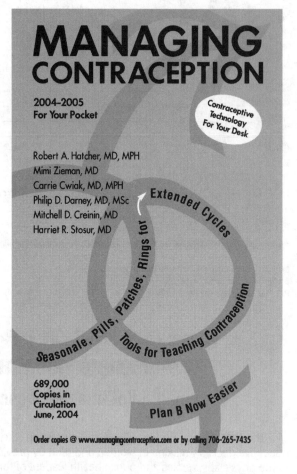

MANAGING CONTRACEPTION

2004–2005
For Your Pocket

Contraceptive Technology For Your Desk

Robert A. Hatcher, MD, MPH
Mimi Zieman, MD
Carrie Cwiak, MD, MPH
Philip D. Darney, MD, MSc
Mitchell D. Creinin, MD
Harriet R. Stosur, MD

Extended Cycles

Seasonale, Pills, Patches, Rings for Tools for Teaching Contraception

Plan B Now Easier

689,000 Copies in Circulation June, 2004

Order copies @ www.managingcontraception.com or by calling 706-265-7435

"I can't adequately express my enthusiasm for the PGTC book. I have rarely found a question that I can't answer by sitting in a patient's room with that book. This has increased the quality of my contraceptive care significantly. Thanks so much!"

Todd Lang, MD
2430 4th Avenue
Altoona, PA 16602

Easily fits into shirt or coat pocket. You will not want to leave home without it!

BRIDGING THE GAP COMMUNICATIONS, INC.

Order online: www.ManagingContraception.com

NOTES

Check out the Q and A's on
www.managingcontraception.com

NOTES

Check out the Q and A's on
www.managingcontraception.com

NOTES

Check out the Q and A's on
www.managingcontraception.com

NOTES

Check out the Q and A's on
www.managingcontraception.com